#iamdone

#iamdone

"There is a shift happening in awareness and consciousness that is disrupting the status quo. And when people experience that shift, their current way of achieving 'success' becomes inadequate and opaque and they're often not sure how to fill this new gap.

They know there is a bigger game and they're ready to play, but they're unsure of the space.

In #iamdone, Amber not only describes the 'space', she also shares how she and a group of other awakened women are playing in that space.

If you've had that shift and you're in the wide open space ... no longer looking for a guru, but looking to share in a collective wisdom ... then I think you'll find something unique for you in this work."

—Dr. Nic Lucas, www.niclucas.com

"#iamdone captures a very vulnerable yet empowering process that so many women are waking up to everyday. After experiencing such highs and lows, we are questioning everything. Nothing is as it was.

I amongst many women have been waiting for this moment when a collective tribe of genius minds bring forth this wisdom into an open conversation and opportunity to walk forward, to create a future for our children that is based on their real needs and an opportunity to be both the genius we are and aligned leaders in our own lives - together.

The old teachings and methodologies will be surpassed by this education and insights. There is no genius in women looking old teachings when the world is a different place. The future requires a new guide and set of collective wisdom, one guru does not have the answers to the new world. Technology must play a role in this. The technology that gives us access to a collective intelligence not experienced before.

Move aside our old teachers who have dominated in the past and allow the collective wisdom of many teach us the beliefs that transcend intellectual insight. This will contribute to our new world, I have no doubt.

Amber McLean writes with such truth, vulnerability and intelligence that will attract those women who already live profound lives but whom seek a tribe to align with to pave the way for a new world. The calling is loud if you choose to listen to it."

—Mia Munro, www.miamunro.com

"There is a huge tide of rising awakened Women leaders who are ready to turn the troubles of this world around.

Amber has created this powerful catalyst that will draw you out of any limitation and help you stand united, with other powerful Women, to uplift your personal and professional life.

This book is more than a feel good story. It will start a fire deep within, which will ignite your deepest passion and radiant gifts.

Let your heart devour this sacred calling."

—Satyen Raja, Founder WarriorSage.com

"In this unique book, Amber McLean opens up the doors to a unique evolutionary portal of much needed wisdom for the woman who is ready to embark on a journey of unlimited freedom, power, sacredness,and self love.

Through its pages, you will experience connection, openness, and a shedding of the old which is needed for the next evolutionary steps of universal evolution.

It is timely, authentic, and needed.

It is not a message of hope.

It is not a motivational speech.

#iamdone is a timely call for the woman who is traveling this journey; to do so by fearlessly embracing once and for all, the full potential of her soul.

Namaste."

—**Ivonne Delaflor, President,**
Delaflor Teachings International
www.EsTiempoDeDespertar.com

#iamdone

Stop Dancing on the Fringes

AMBER McLEAN

NEW YORK

NASHVILLE • MELBOURNE • VANCOUVER

#iamdone
Stop Dancing on the Fringes

Published in New York, New York, by Morgan James Publishing in partnership with Difference Press. Morgan James is a trademark of Morgan James, LLC. www.MorganJamesPublishing.com

The Morgan James Speakers Group can bring authors to your live event. For more information or to book an event visit The Morgan James Speakers Group at www.TheMorganJamesSpeakersGroup.com.

ISBN 9781683504702 paperback
ISBN 9781683504719 eBook
Library of Congress Control Number: 2017902539

Cover Design by:
Heidi Miller

Interior Design by:
Chris Treccani
www.3dogcreative.net

In an effort to support local communities, raise awareness and funds, Morgan James Publishing donates a percentage of all book sales for the life of each book to Habitat for Humanity Peninsula and Greater Williamsburg.

Get involved today! Visit
www.MorganJamesBuilds.com

disclaimer

MY **dedication** TO MY GIRLS

For Avalon and Aria...my greatest teachers and most magnificent students. I love you to the moon and back. Thank you for choosing me as your Mum.

I salute YOU

I salute my Mum & Dad; my protectors, my supporters, my teachers. I chose them, and they have delivered beyond imagination. Their belief in me, is the LIFE FORCE that keeps me blissfully experiencing the extraordinary adventure, that is, my life.

I salute my Husband; my beacon of "best self" light. Always bringing me back to the beauty, truth & lessons of the present moment.

I salute Grandma, Da and the entire McLean clan; potent models of unconditional love + support.

I salute my Ambodhi Sisters; stunning activators of my big crazy insane Vision.

In this life, and the infinite lives ahead…may we continue to bless the planet with our collaborative genius.

table of contents

A foreword
WORTH READING

Written By Clarinda Tivoli-Braun

It was a crisp winter morning in Sydney, Australia. I remember walking up to the office building with my hands in the pockets of my red double-breasted coat, shoulders shrugged to hold the thick bundled scarf close to my ears. I could see my breath as I waited in the small commercial lot, surrounded by lush, South Sydney foliage. I was a fair distance from the hustle and bustle of the city. It was a nice spot, I thought. Quiet and peaceful.

Through the glass doors, I see my client wave, and walk up to let me in. All previous exchanges between us had been via email, so this was the first time meeting in person.

I was a little nervous. This was a high-calibre client - she had a significant following, a strong brand, and although I had confidence in my ability to provide what she needed...she also had a lot to lose.

We were starting three full days together to prepare a sales presentation that she was to present...the following weekend.

Not an easy task, when you're selling what we would call a "soft" product, to a very select market, and at a high price point. Not to mention, (at the time) I would have recommended at least a six-week lead up in preparation for that level of work.

At the end of three days, she had to come out with a well-crafted, high converting presentation, that would bring a significant return to her business. Or...she'd lose three days of crucial event prep time, as well as a significant consulting fee, for nothing.

But I was in my prime. I was ready to bring my best. This was what I knew I was really, really good at. I'd faced far more difficult challenges before, and I took some solace in the fact that I had already produced great results for a myriad of clients at this point...so I had confidence that - so long as we "pushed" - she could get the result she wanted.

She led me down the hall, and into a large boardroom, just for us. True to her go-getter nature, I noticed the work had already begun - paperwork and devices sprawled out on the table, butchers paper and markers on the easel, ready to go. I let down my heavy laptop briefcase, and peeled off the layers to adjust to the warmth inside.

She made sure I was comfortable with a cup of peppermint tea, as I set up next to her. We "small-talked", just enough to break ice, but we didn't waste any time. I opened up my three-day training manual for her on the first page, and we began.

"Want"

Just so you understand the kind of woman this is...

She could have attended a three-day training with me in a small group scenario. Same content, perhaps even better value because of what others bring to the table (and I would have preferred that for her, and for myself, being better leverage) but it wasn't good enough for her. It didn't fit with her dates, she had a deadline, and...she just wanted what she wanted.

So, she chose to spend three times the fee, to have me consult her one-on-one, for three days.

I didn't even have to arrange our venue - she had it arranged, and I just had to show up.

This was a woman, who, no matter what circumstance was thrown at her, she would use her magical scissors (otherwise known as "push", "drive" or "strive") to cut it out in whatever shape she saw fit. No matter the cost, no matter the obstacles - she would make it work...if that's what she wanted. Nothing, and no one would get in the way of that.

This was great news for me - I got a great deal of satisfaction by the successful outcomes of my clients. I knew that the ones who had such character, were the ones who wouldn't let anything get in the way of their successful implementation of what they learnt.

I certainly hoped she wouldn't be any different.

"Push"

We pushed through that first day, and I remember going home to pull off my heels, and massage my feet with my head swelling and spinning.

"One day down, two more to go", I would think to myself as I ate a quick dinner and began to wind down for bed.

It was more taxing than a group training, oddly enough. She put me to work, that's for sure! The pressure of the deadline was burdening.

Each day we would delve deeper into the core of who she was, and its relationship to her product. How her combination of innate gifts, and the unique circumstances in her life prepared her to be this "perfect" solution for her clients-to-be.

It would exhaust us. All of her genius that we "threw up" onto the board-table, then had to go through the often-overwhelming process of elimination, selection, and assembly into a beautifully structured, emotionally moving sales presentation.

Three days passed.

I'm not quite sure how we jam-packed everything we needed to over that short period of time...but we did!

She had more to work on by herself that week before her event, but the necessary structure was there.

Considering the event preparation on top of her day-to-day business dealings, it was a push...but this woman was more than capable.

"Enough"

A couple of weeks had gone by, and I'm ashamed to say I was far too busy in my "busy-ness" to check on her outcome, as I would have liked to. She got in touch, and of course, she blew her presentation out of the water. She had an unusually high conversion of her audience to sales, and was then busy fulfilling the needs of new clients, and meeting the demands that an influx of new business brings.

Hearing this news, for me, was highly satisfying...

But not quite "enough".

What's interesting, is that it wasn't until three years later, that I found out that she had had the same experience.

Amber was highly satisfied with her outcome...

...but not quite "enough".

"Heal"

My beautiful son was born in Hawaii about three years later, in a vastly different phase of life for me. I had packed up and moved to the islands - a dream I had had since I was 12 years old - and met and married the man of my dreams. I spent every available hour dancing as my ancestors did (with Polynesian blood in my veins, the dance, song, and art always held a special place in my heart). I was called to the arts of my ancestors, to heal.

Within the year of my three day training with Amber, I had survived a terrible ordeal with a previous business partner - abuse, wrongful allegations, all in a very public (email broadcasts and social media) setting. Everything collapsed before me. I received ho'ailona (dreams, signs and messages) for years that this would come...but of course, I didn't listen. It was inevitable; I knew that the day would come when I had to stand up for what I felt was right, even if it cost me everything.

I knew the life I was living, then, wasn't "it". Whatever that "niggling" feeling was, caused such mayhem, and destruction in my life.

This began a turbulent journey. I ran as far as I could from the business and personal development circles that I worked and socialised in. Everything and everyone in those worlds reminded me of that torment; everything was painted red, and anything that seemed the least bit inauthentic or out of integrity produced a physical, regurgitative feeling in my stomach.

Depression, ambitious confusion, and the threat of a rare cancer taking over my body ensued. I am so grateful to this day that I had the love and support of my husband, and family, to see me through it all.

When I became pregnant, we miraculously found ourselves in the loving embrace of a local Hawaiian community, who I know were brought to us through the guidance of my ancestors. They cared for me and my husband throughout my pregnancy. They fed us, they did pule (prayer) with us. They taught us about the aina (land) and how it provides for us during pregnancy and birth. They gave us lomi, and prepared my husband in the Hawaiian way of supporting me during labor, and how to deliver our baby. We learnt how to ho'oponopono (reconcile and clear the path) for our keiki's smooth and harmonious entry into the world. They prepared our family not just for our son, but for seven generations ahead of us.

On June 20, 2015, after 3 days of start and stop labor, I went into active labor while on my bed, with a young la'au lapa'au expert (herb healer) sitting behind me, my husband and mum on each side, and an older woman (who many refer to as "Aunty of the islands") eyeing me from another room.

I called for her. I winced, whined, and moaned. "Why isn't he here yet?" I said, giving up my previous strong facade, and about to cry.

She tells me that this is birth. This is the experience. Many women had this experience before me, and now it was my time.

I hated her in this moment. I felt all the anger and disappointment and sadness of recent years bubble up in me.

This was the moment I chose to be "done".

And in a few breaths, I was.

"Done"

"Hey there dear Clarinda, I'm not sure if you remember me..."

Uh oh. Here we go... I thought, as I continued to read this email, while nursing my 7 week old son.

This woman had "an idea", and she wanted my help.

Something about "self-evolution", and liberation.

"Activating unimaginable human potential", she said.

Sounded like some B.S. I'd heard and seen A MILLION TIMES before.

I was NOT interested. I was flattered, that she thought of me! But...not interested. I didn't want to touch that with a 10-foot pole.

Besides, what was her REAL agenda anyway? What was her end game here?

I was not about to interrupt the beautiful sanctuary that I had created, that was my family, to help some lacklustre personal development start up for someone from my tainted past life.

So I let it sit in my inbox for a day or two. I went back and re-read it a few times.

Glimpses of optimism and my curiosity grew, calling me to at least give her the benefit of the doubt, and hear more about it.

Doesn't hurt to hear her out, right?

I replied, reluctantly, and agreed to have a chat over Skype.

I sat in my home office, that I hadn't unpacked since we bought the house and had it freshly painted just a few weeks before baby was born. Surrounded by boxes, but with this unbelievably awe-inspiring view of the tallest mountain on Oahu, I sat and connected with this woman, catching up on recent years.

It just so happened, we had oddly similar stories to tell. So odd, in fact, that I almost felt like she was tailoring her stories to sound more like mine.

I would tell her (as if it was a warning), "Life is REALLY different for me now".

She would reply "I get it. Me too". But I didn't believe that she really "got it".

I was polite. I told her that I've just become a mum, I was still figuring that "new parent" life out, and that I was open to having further conversations, to get to know the depth of the project, the intentions, her needs, expectations, and how her and I might fit in it all.

She had complete respect and understanding for where I was at, and the need for further conversation.

We spent about five weeks getting to know each other - the new "selves" that we'd become. I learnt about her project, and although it appeared like many other projects I'd come across before, there was something "different" to this. Couldn't quite put my finger on it - and I wasn't certain if it was just my glimpses of optimism.

The conversations were enjoyable - it was actually really freeing, refreshing and inspiring to engage in these interactions over our very unique set of life circumstances that we had both found ourselves in.

We reflected on the lessons in the ugliness of our pasts, and we relished in the bliss and wonder of the lives we'd created for ourselves and our families…"by some miracle".

Moreover, she says she has a WHOLE GROUP OF WOMEN who share this experience. Women just like us - successful, burnt, dragged through the mud, and re-birthed anew. I hardly believed it.

Maybe they had "similar experiences" …but surely, not like "me", I thought.

But I was running out of time. I learned all that I needed to, to make a decision.

On the fifth week, a few days before my final call with her, I was messaging my older sister Philadelphia who lives in Europe. She asked how I was going, and what was the latest with her favourite nephew!

I relaxed into my rocking chair with baby in my lap as she told me how the sale of her business was going, and I shared with her that I had a potential client that I wasn't sure if I wanted to take on or not.

"Why?" She asks.

"Well, it's kind of a personal development start up. And I'm all for that, but I've seen a million times how the lines can get blurred with a growing PD business - the conflict between their new age philosophies and the practical business needs. And I'm not entirely sure of her real intentions, or her level of integrity. I just have a real problem with people who say they have good intentions…and then don't."

To which she replies (in classic Philly style), "Hey, I'll take that client if she's selling baby unicorns, but that's me! I don't have the snooty moral standards that you do!"

I shake my head and laugh...

"Damn my snooty morals, I'd be on a yacht off of Cannes if I didn't have those!"

She replied sarcastically, "Exactly! And now look at you. Living in Hawaii with a loving husband and a baby bear. You done messed up."

Touché, sis.

But just as I think she couldn't offer any real advice, besides a good laugh, she says, "Think of it this way. If you ARE involved, you can make sure it's not a fluffy scam jam."

Fluffy scam jam... Yup. I'd come across a few of those before.

I'm not sure if it was what she said, or just the permission it gave me, but when Amber asked if I'd like to work with her a few days later, I said YES.

"Crack"

I was NOT "all in" on this. I was prepared to over-deliver to Amber, of course, but I wasn't so "in love" with the project, that I had to involve myself personally. I was passionate about helping her to have the impact she wanted, and that she was helping others to do the same, in their own ways. I would consult on this, from afar, and at some point get some kind of satisfaction that her and the group would benefit, and go out to do great work in the world.

But me? No. I wasn't about to join this group. I wasn't like them. At least I didn't think I was. And it's not like she was trying to "sell me" on it anyway - which semi-confirmed for me that I wasn't "one of them".

Amber did ask me, however, to be a guest speaker at one of her Australian retreats (via Skype from Hawaii, since I had a newborn), to which I accepted.

As the date came close, I was concerned that I didn't know the group of ladies well enough to be able to tailor the content to them specifically.

She says "I tell you what - I'll just add you into the group online, so you can see all of our interactions, and feel free to participate as little or as much as you like."

I hesitated. "It's okay, that might not be necessary..."

"-I'll just add you in", she insists.

Amber welcomes me in, and I feel this rush of love and support from this group of women who didn't know me - but it was as if they did. It felt like a "welcome back", or a "good to have you home, sister"

It was a bit odd. A bit cultish. All peace, love and mung beans. And I respected that...but it wasn't something I could bear to be in for too long, I thought.

I introduced myself - a quick rundown of my expertise, my involvement in the project, and my story and personal experiences of recent years that sent me on an inward journey. I only did that because Amber suggested I do it - I wasn't keen on opening up to these ladies I didn't know, without provocation.

Their responses, although loving, seemed...naive. Premature.

They made it seem like they all knew what I went through, had seen all of that ugliness for themselves, and not only did they accept me for it, but they revered my entire journey. Like all of that hardship was some kind of accolade. War scars to be proud of. Proof I was on a "heroine's journey".

How could they possibly know what I went through? There's no one like me. No one understands what I went through. Clearly, they didn't get it.

Over the coming weeks, I get to know each of them intimately, as they vulnerably share their inward journeys, as and when "life" comes up for them - all the while simultaneously, showing up in the world with big projects, big intentions, big promises.

As part of my research for the project, I personally interviewed a number of these ladies, searching for the commonalities in their stories, experiences, behaviours.

These women didn't mess around.

They were huge successes in their own right - they had their own significant followings - we had several authors, artists, most were speakers, some with "past lives" on the top of corporate ladders, and high-level practitioners in health, spirituality, business and marketing. One lady was all that AND was a pilot about to circumnavigate the globe, for goodness sakes.

Observing the vulnerable sharing within this group was like seeing a famous singer on stage, and then having the curtains and backstage walls removed. I would see them perform for their audiences, and then I would see them retreat to their green rooms at interval - have a drink, nourish themselves. There was no interval music to keep the energy up, no "posturing", no facade. They would light up a cigarette and peel off the makeup, eyelashes, wigs, and change into a new costume. I would see them at their weakest, at their darkest, at their lows of doubt and harsh self-criticism. The public didn't get to see this - but I did.

And they all felt safe to do this, because they were all on equal footing. It was like they were "blood sisters" - they'd been sworn in to keep utmost confidentiality, and support each other in the way they would want for themselves.

AND...Amber was not separate from this. She interacted as they did, supported as they did, and didn't censor her journey, didn't hold back, nor did she hide, in any "pedestal-like" effort to seem "elevated" among them. The only visible "leader" in this space, was each individual's highest self - their highest intelligence, and what they would call their "wise woman".

Again and again I would hear them praise the dynamic of the space - the technology that supported it, the methodology, the calibre of women they shared it with.

"I know I'm not alone anymore", they would say. "I can finally be ME."

And that would seem to be just as important as the huge emotional, spiritual, and/or creative breakthroughs they would experience in a matter of moments, all in their combined support of each and everyone's individual wisdom.

As the weeks and months went on, I felt the urge to engage - to relate - to plug in, as there were times I knew I could contribute uniquely like in no other space...and be impacted, like in no other space.

But no - I can't do that, I thought. I can't become "vulnerable" in their eyes. And I must separate myself to remain "objective", so as to do my best work as a consultant on the project.

Well, that was partially true. But it was mostly my B.S excuse.

Crack...crack...crack.

The Ambodhi chisel on my ice cold resistance ensued.

All that I thought I was sure about was slowly, and lovingly, being challenged in the background of my work.

I continued to consult and support Amber and the project as best I could...but I couldn't hold out any longer.

"Flipped"

I'm not even sure I can describe how my world is different now.

My short time in the space has felt like a loving eternity.

And guess what?

My work was not, at all, compromised by my vulnerability. Go figure...

Sure - I'm braver, I'm more creative. I'm tuned in spiritually and intelligently in the unique way I know my ancestors were, and all on a daily basis. But that's not even the biggest takeaway.

I thought I was out here to make a difference. Profound consulting work that served others in a deeply life-altering way. And that's the dynamic that I thought my success relied upon.

Amber, and Ambodhi, like NO OTHER client, has made me question every interaction. My entire approach. What's odd is that it's not necessarily any different, but it feels flipped on its side - like we're experiencing it from another dimension - with its own new set of endless possibilities.

And it's not by anything that anyone said! It's just what happens in the presence of "what" this thing IS and continues to BE.

There is something very curious about this space.

"Fulfilled"

I'm not sure who you are, what unique story and experiences you harbour, or what events have lead you to be reading this book.

What I do know is that "destiny" pulls you out to experience what it holds for you, in one way or another. Yes, we're master creators of our lives, and yes, we have the freedom of will, and choice.

But sometimes, as the ambitious women that we are, we can stretch that luxury of will and choice well past the point of usefulness and benefit.

We get in the way of ourselves...I know you know that.

I'm not going to tell you what to do, or what to think, because if this book has made it into your hands, then you're wise and evolved enough to come to your own intelligent conclusions.

So I'll just share this:

The #iamdone project came into my life as a distraction for me to "stay busy" - to feel like I'm having an impact - to fulfil my "ego self".

But what was truly happening, was it was here to impact ME.

So this time, the outcome has been not just highly satisfying...but truly unimaginably MORE than "enough".

And I know Amber is sharing that experience as well.
Enjoy the read...
Aloha

THE whisper

"I am done dimming my whole self, to fit in.

I am done with the illusion of limitation.

I am done with dancing around the fringes of my meaningful work.

I am done believing I have to be perfect, just because I'm an authority figure.

I am done with pedestals and believing "they are better than me".

I am done believing my genius has no value.

I am done with not being fully self-expressed.

I am done believing I have to choose between my professional ambitions and my spiritual growth.

I am done hiding my vulnerability.

I am done playing small.

I am done with the spiritual work without the action.

I am done recycling through the same lessons over and over."

- The Ambodhi Alliance

In May 2014, I heard the whisper "I am done".

I thought this declaration trickled from the intricate neural wiring in my brain. But I now know, it was in fact, a message from Higher Self.

You're reading this book, because you've also heard these three words whispered in your being.

It's my belief, that the moment you verbalised this whisper of "I am done", you unconsciously answered the call to RISE UP into your next dimension of growth...your next dimension of impact.

And what divine timing it is, for this almighty rise in growth and impact to occur...because just like us, you have wildly important, meaningful shit to bless the planet.

Know that this Whisper is a promise of an unimaginable power entering your life.

Know also, that you are not alone.

Thousands of women all over the world are gathering around the whisper of #iamdone, with the intention of activating collective human potential.

(Simply type this hashtag into your search engines and join the conversation).

WE ARE
done

We are wildly ambitious, awakened women, who are totally done dancing on the fringes.

Dancing on the fringes of our absolute potential.

On the fringes of our extraordinary growth.

On the fringes of our most meaningful important work.

And most of all, we are done dancing on the fringes of our greatest impact.

You have a deep KNOWING, that to lead, inspire and influence meaningful, sustainable change, you MUST grow beyond the limitations of your epigenetic and genetic programming…

Those deeply embedded, un-resourceful belief systems that are keeping you STUCK in a life that feels diluted in meaning, growth and contribution.

Like you, I have outgrown conventional personal and professional development, as a stand alone approach.

So, inspired by an unconventional idea…

I gathered 17 women (whom are just you and I), to discover how this concept could support our desire to transcend our un-resourceful programming and activate our absolute potential.

We've spent two years building and testing "this alternative". And what we've discovered is unique, multi-faceted AND wildly profound.

We know it's not just the 18 of us whom have been dancing on the fringes…

Whom have been teetering between two significant themes of life: Progression and Potency (which we'll get into shortly)…

And whom have important work to do.

So consider this book a divine instrument; uniting this unique body of work, with you, the woman it's destined to activate.

ʻTHE idea

"I knew it was incredibly powerful, but because of its complexity and multi-dimensional layers, I needed to dig deep into my unconscious so I could articulate what it was."

In 2012 I had an idea that was inspired by my daughter Avalon; she was two at the time and I was madly (and that's a nice way to describe it!) running my business.

I was a marketing mentor for women business owners and I was working 60-70 hours a week.

I was burnt out. I was a bitch to be around. I was unhealthy. My relationship with my husband was strained, but I loved helping women grow. I loved helping them expand. I loved helping them find their true value and that really drove me every day to keep driving and striving and building my business.

One evening, while preparing dinner, I asked Avalon to do something (I can't remember what), and what she did next, will remain etched in my mind FOREVER.

Avalon was sitting down at her little table and chairs, with her play computer and toy phone. She had her back to me and before I could finish my sentence, Avalon interrupted with a raised (stop talking) hand and said "I'm very busy at the moment."

Holy shit!

I came to realise that I had been choosing to sacrifice everything in my life, in order to achieve my goals…and this was causing me to become more and more disconnected from my daughter.

I knew in that moment that I needed to take responsibility for this so called "Life" I was creating.

I needed to step up and be accountable for how I was showing up on the planet; who I was being.

Laying in bed that night, while regurgitating the event in my mind and wallowing in guilt, I suddenly realised that I didn't want to marinate in this bullshit space anymore.

That's when this "idea" came to me.

I thought to myself, instead of being "in a puddle" each night, I could keep a journal of my observed "less than best self" behaviours. And with the intention of bringing more presence, gratitude and growth into our lives, I could share these journal entries with Avalon.

Over several months, this simple idea evolved into something so completely unique, highly complex and significantly profound…

The evolution of this idea stoked the "desire fire" I had a burning within me, and this yearning prompted me to reach out and connect with Dr. Nic Lucas (who is now one of my dearest mentors, colleagues and supporters).

It was a Tuesday afternoon. Nic and I had never met, so this would be our very first conversation. We chatted on Skype for about 45 minutes, mostly about this idea. I can remember feeling a little embarrassed about my woeful description of this concept. I was honestly struggling to describe what it was... because in reality, I really didn't know. But Nic saw through my clumsy explanation, and immediately understood the Vision I had. In fact, it was only several minutes into our discussion, that Nic knew exactly how he could support me, this crazy woman, with a wild idea, who was asking for help...but didn't know what kind of help.

This divine "helping hand" that Nic extended to me, came in the form of a short story...

He told me about a research project which required him to interview various people, asking them questions about themselves. He would then get the interviews transcribed, so he could read and highlight sections of their answers that exposed what they believed about themselves.

He then shared these "perceptions of Self" with each of the individuals who took part in the interviews. And what Nic observed next, deeply intrigued me...

Nic proceeded to tell me, that these interview participants couldn't believe the "descriptions" Nic was reflecting back to them. They thought Nic had written these in "his" words.

What Nic taught me that day, was the power of "observation". And even more profound, the power of learning about yourself FROM yourself.

This conversation with Nic, convinced me, that this concept was even more powerful than I had imagined…and that I needed to pursue it.

One Tuesday afternoon, I was on a monthly "catch-up" call with my dear friends and colleagues, Michelle Cannan and Mia Munro.

We were sharing the "discomfort" of being authority figures within a coaching and mentoring industry we didn't resonate with anymore…and what our hearts and souls yearned for instead.

I can't remember what I said, but whatever it was, prompted Mia to ask me "if you knew you only had 12-months left on this planet, how would you be contributing to the planet?"

When I heard this question…I felt a massive blanket of relief engulf my entire body!

It was if Mia asking this question, gave me permission to JUMP head first into this unknown space. And despite feeling scary, this space felt far more f'ing EXPANSIVE than the life I was currently "operating" within.

That was it.

I decided that I had to give this a go. I had to go all in on this concept, on this idea I had.

So I took the BIG LEAP!

I gathered an incredible collection of women known now as, The Ambodhi Alliance; 17 women, whom were just like me; ambitious, "successful" AND awakened.

"We are not just a spiritual or consciousness awareness group, there's also a lot of ambition.

We've got world changers in the group, and I'm a very ambitious woman; I've got a lot of work to do here on the planet right now, as we all do.

Everyone in the group has that same drive. There is a really strong balance between spirituality and consciousness; between awakening your inner gifts and your expression of those gifts; taking action, getting out there in the world and using that wisdom, awareness, insight and understanding to serve and create change."

Kylie Ryan - Ambodhi Alliance Foundation Member

We are consultants, performing artists, authors, advisors, speakers, thought leaders.

We are intensely interested in the inner workings of peak human performance, and soak ourselves in the wisdom of energetic healing, spiritual awakening, quantum physics, neurolinguistic programming, cellular biology, human psychology, entrepreneurialism and movement-making.

ᵀᴴᴱ WOMen

We have experienced success according to society's (and perhaps our) definitions but the fulfilment around this success felt hollow.

We are natural born MASSIVE action-takers, so therefore naturally operate from our masculine.

We are a bit intense at times, people can sometimes struggle to keep up with us.

We are high achievers who invest at a high level when it comes to our personal and professional growth.

We love to connect under the context of collaboration (getting BIG meaningful shit done quicker and with more peace, ease and grace).

We're not huge believers in the ideology that we have a specific Life Purpose outside of LOVE. We believe our businesses, our projects, our "work" is simply an expression of LOVE, packaged and delivered via our genius.

I believe we have ALL been assigned the identical Life's Purpose.

In what form this contract of world service manifests, is determined by ego, and how our individual ego's thirst (in that phase of life) needs to be quenched. For it's my belief, that when our ego is "fulfilled", our true Life's Purpose can be fulfilled...

Being LOVE, growth, acceptance, abundance and gratitude. And when we can connect our earthly gifts and talents (ego) with this "way of being"...we will effortlessly make potent impact on humanity.

We are not into the whole "spiritual masturbation" thing. Sitting "in" the work doesn't float our boats...we bliss out on "being" the work.

If there's a lack of action, we get easily bored in the woo-woo, in the stillness.

"Before I found this tribe, there was a lack of a space in my life where I felt that there was an awakened consciousness WITH a purpose."

Kylie Ryan - Ambodhi Alliance Foundation Member

We feel like life is a living death, when it's void of adventure, exploration, unconditional love and a big hairy audacious PROJECT.

We come from all different parts of the world, from all different backgrounds, and vibrate all kinds of different magic; but the one unifying thing that brings us all together, is this...

We DO NOT wish to lead our children down the same re-cycled paths of their generations past.

We believe our children are worthy of learning how to live their most potent life. To create, innovate and lead, by un-apologetically being the full expression of their absolute potential.

We KNOW that we are responsible for fostering this potential, not just through our words, achievements or Empires, but also through our deeds.

Like us, you have decided that your Legacy isn't what you do, it isn't the Empires or Movements that you build, nor the material possessions and creations that you leave on the planet, BUT INSTEAD...

The energy you project, as you fulfil this meaningful work.

We are being called to enhance greater humanity, with the vibrational frequency of our absolute potential. And to fulfil this calling (that we've had since we were so very little), WE are now committed to being the full expression of this.

After my first daughter was growing from a toddler into a child, I began to notice just how much she was modelling me.

Here I was, building a business with the intention of serving others AND to create financial freedom for myself, and my family.

I truly, madly, deeply wanted to provide my family with unlimited choice. I didn't want to be at the mercy of the government, corporate or society's status quo. And I was doing this by trying to fill "voids in my life". Chasing what I perceived I didn't have AND obsessing over what I thought I needed.

In the process, I was physically burning out, I was disconnected from my husband, less and less present with Avalon and unplugging from the precious people, places, events and things in my life.

I was so focused on the destination...the outcome...that I had totally disregarded and disrespected "the process".

Meanwhile...what was my daughter learning, modelling from?

She certainly wasn't forming her beliefs, habits and actions solely from my visions, goals and outcomes.

She was learning from WHO I was being as I was "doing" life.

This was a big turning point for me...and certainly influenced my leap into a steep learning curve, when it came to living a more conscious aware life.

As I became more aware of WHO I was being...and observing the consequences of the my decisions, I was also became aware of the belief and behavioural patterns that were genetically and epigenetically handed down to me.

I came to realise that my programmed belief in lack, scarcity, un-deservedness and unworthiness, was causing me to "re-play the same cycles". Outcomes, results, consequences that my ancestors had cycled through before me.

This programming was installed to keep me safe...to protect me from the dangers of the past.

But the dangers of the past didn't exist in my present moment. Nor did they exist in my daughter's present moment.

This programming was no longer needed.

It had come time for me to STOP these archaic cycles.

THE
un-earthing

So, I was all in on this project. I knew that it was incredibly powerful, but because of its complexity and multi-dimensional layers, I needed to dig deep into my unconscious so I could articulate what it was.

I approached a beautiful soul called Clarinda Tivoli Braun, (whom I had worked with in my "previous life") to ask for her help.

Clarinda's genius, allows you to find, from the depths of your unconscious, the potent magic that sits in the space between your genius and your BIG meaningful work.

It was for this reason, that I asked her to help me uncover what this beautiful collaboration truly was.

Clarinda was very protective of her gifts and as a result, spent 5 weeks connecting deeper into who I was at the core of my being, uncovering my intention behind leading this

"Mission" and whether these two "parts" of me aligned with her values.

To this day, I am eternally grateful that our values aligned. On our third day of working together, Clarinda asked me…

"What are these women experiencing in their lives?

How did they get where they are now?

Where have they been?

Where are they going?

What are their common collective experiences? What are their beliefs and motivations?

How do their external worlds relate to each other and how are these elements of themselves different from the rest of the planet?"

These were really BIG, extremely important questions. Because the answers to these questions were going to unveil what this Mission (I had been called to lead) really was.

So for the following eight months, we went to work, unearthing the unique, complex and multifaceted answers to these beautiful questions.

What we discovered was a phenomenon, we call "Life Themes".

life
THEMES

"Understanding these themes helped us make sense of it all; it helped us understand exactly where we were at and where we were inevitably headed."

When we discovered this phenomenon of Life Themes, it was like a wave of relief that came over us - understanding these themes helped us make sense of it all; it helped us understand exactly where we were at and where we were inevitably headed.

There's three Life Themes that we progress through in our lives. These three Life Themes are...

Permanence, Progression + Potency.

Each theme represents an "apprenticeship" in human evolution.

Each of these Life Themes have specific desires and motivations, they have specific belief systems and they have a specific external environmental architecture (people, places, events and things).

Each of these Life Themes are embodied by us, by certain vibrational frequency ranges. As we rise up through the Life Themes, our frequency rises. The frequency of our beliefs rise, the vibration of our motivations rise and our potential to create exponential growth and potent impact rises.

What also rises is the complexity and the level of support we need, to connect our internal resources with our external resources…our Ego with Higher Self (more on this later).

permanence

Permanence is simply about surviving this human experience; to believe and behave in a way that allows us to survive on this planet for as long as possible.

The first moment I held Avalon in my hands was <u>the most</u> mind-bending moment. The first thought that came to me when I saw her, was how vulnerable she was to life and how important I was in keeping her safe and loved.

This beautiful part of life as newborn babies represents the commencement of our Life Theme of Permanence.

This Life Theme of Permanence is an incredibly important part of our evolution; it determines our longevity on the planet. Every day we are focused on ensuring our survival. And everyday, our fight or flight instincts are hard at work, keeping us out of danger…keeping us safe.

Our needs within Permanence are very basic, i.e., food, water, comfort and safety.

And as a tribe, we shifted out of Permanence a long time ago.

I remember a moment when I was five years old, living in Bougainville, Papua New Guinea.

I spent a lot of time in my room listening to music, dancing, singing and playing schools.

On this particular day, I remember looking out the window, looking at the banana palms we had outside and asking myself...

"Why aren't I a banana palm?
Why aren't I the grass on the ground?
Why aren't I the flowers in that bush?
Why am I me?
Why have I been chosen to be a human?"

I was really quite perplexed.

It was in that moment, my consciousness kicked in It was that event that sparked my desire to understand how I fitted into this extraordinary environment that was...Life!

This memory may also represent my everlasting shift out of Permanence. A moment in time where I had mastered my physiological, safety-driven needs. The moment I rose into my Life Theme of Progression.

progression

Our Life Theme of "Progression" is based upon exploring the world around us, discovering who we are, how we want to operate in this life and what we want to create.

In this Life Theme, we <u>must</u> progress as humans. And this means everything we do, everything we say and every decision we make, has an impact on our lives and on the lives of those around us.

"Within Progression we have BIG visions, but there's still a lot of external validation.

We are internally driven to experience pleasure and externally driven to avoid pain, so we're willing to lean into challenges; take on the world.

There's lots of doing, and there's a lot of wanting that work to matter, and that means that people must see your work."

Kylie Ryan - Ambodhi Alliance Foundation Member

In Progression, our physiological and safety needs are being fulfilled, and we seek to have other, more ego-driven needs met.

Growth

It's in this phase of life where we're heavily investing in coaches, mentors, training programs. We're constantly scanning for resources that are going to allow us to grow and evolve into our best selves. Modelling is a very important part of this phase and we idolise these teachers, we put them up on pedestal.

"I believed I needed experts to tell me the right way to do it."

Mandy Hargreaves - Ambodhi Alliance Foundation Member

Leverage

We are focused on winning, succeeding, bettering ourselves so that we could be the best. Constantly seeking people, places, events and things that could contribute to our success and growth. Leverage was a really important focus for us. We wanted to know how we could create optimum results with the limited time and resources we had available.

"I was always looking for how to be better while at the same time, being distracted by the bright, shiny object."

Simone Outteridge - Ambodhi Alliance Foundation Member

Up-skilling

We were focused on serving others with the skills we thought we had to be good at (not what we are brilliant it).

Winning

We were almost always operating from our masculine energy and our measurement of success was based on the acknowledgement we received from others. We were deeply committed and ambitious about serving others, but had an ulterior motive; to win, to succeed and to receive recognition.

When I was growing up, my dad's opinion really mattered to me. The way I connected with my dad was through my performance on the sporting field.

My dad loved sport and was incredibly competitive. I believed from a very young age, that when I won, I would receive BIG love from dad. And I did (of course)!

So, I then grew up believing, that when I won, I was worthy of love.

I can see now, how that need to be acknowledged, in order to be loved, influenced my decisions and therefore, my results.

Perfection

It's in this Life Theme of Progression, that we truly begin to wake up. In this phase of life, our muscle of self-awareness really starts to build; however, we are a very harsh judge of ourselves and as a result, push ourselves to the limit (trying to be perfect, to be RIGHT, to be the best). This becomes incredibly exhausting.

For example, for the first 5 years of Avalon's life, I would lay in bed most nights, wallowing in the guilt of how I had interacted with her during that previous day; harshly judging myself as a "bad" mother.

Acknowledgement

We have another exhausting behavioural characteristic in our Life Theme of Progression, i.e., our need to make an impact on others AND to be acknowledged for it. This acknowledgement, this need for validation, is a dominant characteristic of this Life Theme.

> *"What it was like before was a lot of trying to be somebody I wasn't; trying to be somebody that had it all perfect. Trying to be somebody that ticked all the boxes, got all the gold stars, got permission and got acceptance in a box; in a square cube that I knew I didn't fit in."*
>
> ***Tammy Guest - Ambodhi Alliance Foundation Member***

Status

During Progression, we embody the belief that to make a massive impact on the planet, on humanity, we have to shout loud, we have to have a big message, that we need to have a high profile.

Going BIG

On top of that, we also have this insatiable need for cathartic change. We are seeking big transformations, and in the process, we overlook the golden lessons that shine in the understated moments.

Bright + Shiny

It's in this period of life that we slowly became aware of, and even begin plugging into, our natural genius. But despite this, we are also undervaluing it. It comes too easy, therefore it doesn't feel "bright and shiny"…therefore, it doesn't feel "valuable".

I remember when one of my clients, Sam, told me that the GREATEST gift she had received from us working together, was the fact that she had connected into her greatest value. She said this was greater than any monetary result.

Was I proud of this?

I really wasn't.

I was too focused on "what I wanted to be good at" rather than the value I was "effortlessly" providing.

My genius was screaming at me. And I was totally ignoring it.

BETWEEN

then
⁺now

Life in our period of "Progression", compared to life now, in our Life Theme of Potency, is so, so different.

The human experience we are living now, is the most profound period of our lives to date.

But it wasn't a smooth transition.

In fact, I describe this "evanescent period" of life, as a "crazy glitch in my reality".

And before we dive into this "transitory chasm", we'd like to share with you, particular events that occurred in our lives.

Human experiences that we now know were, THE CALL.

The call to rise up into a higher vibrational experience of life…into a higher realm of consciousness.

THE call

These calls, to rise into a higher consciousness, were expressed as all sorts of burn out and break down.

These experiences caused us to stop, turn and face the choices we had made.

What we know now is, it needed to get worse before it got better. We needed to demolish the veils covering our darkest shadows, before we could rebuild and rise into our absolute potential.

MY
calling

"They accused me of being a FRAUD and threatened to take me to court."

I had attracted the most extraordinary collection of women into my high-end mentoring Program. All had the same desire; to grow their businesses. However, at the same time, this tribe of women were two sub-groups that represented two different intentions.

I had one group of women who came to grow their business and were deeply curious about how they could grow in the process, while the other group of women simply wanted to influence and impact as many people as possible...with the greatest leverage possible.

The reality was, I had attracted the two "parts" of myself, that were in conflict. One part of me loved playing in my magic, while the other part rejected it, doing what I thought I needed to do, to impact as many people as possible while building wealth.

Within that program there were moments I was in flow and having a ball. But this was only occurring when I was engaged with one particular group.

When serving the other group, the experience felt painful, exhausting and heavy.

I remember going to sleep some nights thinking, "What have I created? I don't want to get up in the morning and keep doing this."

I had a high-level of revenue flowing into the bank but it was heartbreaking. I'd have these moments of flow and then these moments of high resistance, pain, exhaustion and frustration.

It was that period of my life that sparked my "calling".

Six weeks later; while my husband was in China on a business trip, I woke one to find a scathing FB post inside my private client Facebook group. Inside this post, my longest loyal client had shared how deeply upset she was at me, my process, and the fact that she believed I had SOLD her a service that didn't work. And another one of my clients also joined in on the conversation.

One said "you're a very good salesperson - selling me what you thought I wanted to hear". She described me as being "the same as all the others", referring to other mentors and coaches in the marketplace whom had "stolen her money".

Another sent me an email, asking me to repay her Program fees, and threatened to take me to court in the US, if I did not refund her money. Her reason: I promised her an outcome she did not produce, therefore, I had sold her a fraudulent service.

Another client got her bank to contact my financial institution, to inform them that I had fraudulently charged her credit card and demanded I return the funds.

Within 7 days, $60,000 had been wiped from my bottom line but even more painful, was the attack on my character.

I too was disillusioned with the quality of coaching and mentoring that was being offered in my industry. This fuelled my commitment to deliver THE highest quality service and facilitate the highest quality outcome for my clients.

And it appeared that I had created the total opposite of this, in the eyes of these women.

I was crushed.

I can only describe the weeks that followed as torturous. And my persistent compulsion to "bitch & moan" about these events (with the humans in my life who fed my "victim"), caused the pain to amplify.

It seems that "my perception of reality", during those weeks, was dull life tones. Like the world around me was muted...and all I could hear, was the blood-thirsty war going on inside my head.

I felt intense emotions of sadness, anger and fear.

I was sad that I wasn't experiencing life the way I thought I should have been to this point.

I was angry that I'd worked so f'ing hard to get to a place where my business was the master of me and I was totally afraid that I was squandering the time that I had left on this planet to make a meaningful impact on my daughter's life, on her belief systems and on her visions for her life.

I was totally numb.

I don't remember where I was, what day it was, or what had been the "final" trigger, but I do remember falling to me knees, with my head in my lap...crying. My body was experiencing a sensational pain that I hadn't experienced before.

I was mourning.

Mourning a part of me that had suffered a long & painful death.

In that moment, on the floor in my lounge roo m, I was mourning the death of purpose.

A moment of no return.

I had nothing to stand up and face, but mySelf...absent of purpose. Absent of "life".

I was deeply hurt by the event.

I was sad, confused, overwhelmed, angry.

I had no idea which road I was going to take, but I knew it was either giving up and walking away from my business OR going ALL IN!

CLARINDA'S calling

"*I found out I had a miscarriage. Within a whirlwind of a few days, I found out that it wasn't just a miscarriage...I had a tumour*"

Clarinda Tivoli-Braun - Ambodhi Alliance Foundation Member

I was knocked down severely. I owned this big training business that had me touring all the main cities in Australia, non-stop. It was a business that was all about authenticity, being true to self. It was based on teaching people how to bring their real selves to the stage, and not have to be anybody else, copy anybody else's model, system, scripts or swipes; but to be able to speak from the heart - and do it in a strategic way that can benefit you in your business.

It was about deeply uncovering the true essence of your message, and then being able to meet the market with communications (primarily through speech and copy) that was supported to do so, with congruency and integrity.

So it was all based on this beautiful foundation. If I look back now, that was me living at TWO PERCENT of my full expression and where I really wanted to go with it. At the time I felt like that was "it". We were the "bee's knees"; and that business and who I was in it, was such a big part of my identity.

That all went to shambles for many reasons - it was quite the ordeal. I trace the reason back to this: myself and my business partner at the time really..."grew into ourselves".

I became much more of myself, and he became much more of himself. We were essentially very different and had vastly different ideas as to how we wanted to maintain and grow that business.

Pile on top of that, there was a lot of emotional abuse, manipulation and very sketchy stuff going on financially that I was just too busy to see was going on. I was just SO passionate about the work, so all my focus was on our "babies", our clients, and I had 53 or 54 that I had to work with one-on-one, to make sure they all had lots of love and attention.

It boggles my mind now to think I had that kind of workload, because I live a very different life now.

So even though we had these beautiful philosophies, we were having internal conflicts that were not congruent with those philosophies at all.

For those reasons and many more, everything crumbled before me. That was such a big part of my identity - it was my ego - I was very attached to every part of that business.

As I started to find out what was going on, my partner at the time couldn't go down "gracefully". He went down clawing and attacking all the way, so I took the brunt of that. There were lots of false accusations made against me, and my whole reputation and credibility was, I felt, ruined. It didn't matter who was favoured in the legal battle - it came down to an exhausting PR game with clients, and the damage had been done. My innocence and ego really took a knock.

At the time, it felt so disastrous and I didn't know how I was going to come back out of it - but that was an event that was destined to pull me toward my greater "calling", because that was me living a very diluted version of my fully expressed self.

That event was then followed by a whole host of events that was essentially the "divine bus" that kept coming to hit me just as I would gain a little bit of strength to feel like I could "do" something.

I was very intelligent, I knew I could strategise and execute many amazing ideas, so I thought, "I just have to plan this out, and I'm going to move forward."

It was very difficult to get to that space in the first place. I was swept into a very deep depression. Thank goodness for small mercies, I had a loving husband and family who were behind me 200%.

I remember times when I was in bed with four or five big thick folders around me doing accounting and trying to pick up the pieces.

I'd wake up with all of this around me and I would just do only what I had to, to survive, really, that day. I would get up at some point and butter some bread and put a bit of honey on it and that would be all that I'd eat.

Then I'd go back and crawl up into bed and just do whatever I could which was...barely anything. I was so weak and just emotionally a wreck. To start to feel any strength to come up out of bed was a miracle, so I wanted to put that strength to good use, and wanted to move forward and do something; take big actions. And I certainly did. I took many. Until...

There was a particular time I decided to write this big long email in defence of all of the attacks that were made against me. I was about to click 'send' on it and I thought, "No, I'll just step back from the laptop and take a break, and come back later and see if I want to still send it, or edit it, perhaps".

I stepped out to take a dance class. I live here in Hawaii now (which, by the way, was something else that I was being called towards over this journey).

I travelled to Hawaii to take holidays every now and then. I would just find such bliss in the silence, in the creative side of myself that I could express in Hawaii. I came to Hawaii to dance, which was so healing for me, and what I needed to heal the burnout.

I began to find more of my true self was starting to leak. So I was writing that email, about to click 'send'; I stepped away from the computer and went to go take a dance class. I got on my little moped and drove around the corner. On the way, I barely even remember what happened; I just went right into the back of a three-car collision in front of me. I bounced of the Jeep in front of me and went flying.

The next thing I remember I was on the ground, trying to get up, but I couldn't. Bystanders were running towards me. The ambulance came and I spent the night in the hospital. Nothing was broken, thankfully, but I was so heavily bruised that I couldn't walk well for about ten days, so I was given crutches.

Again, I got this little bit of strength and I was about to send this very bold email, but then I got knocked down. I barely even remembered there was an email in my drafts folder. I cancelled my appointments and calls for the next couple of weeks, and I just STOPPED. I lay in bed every day and furthered my depression, that I thought I was coming out of.

I just had to stop and listen. That was obviously telling me to not send that email, and just chill out. It's not time for action yet, and it's not worth it. None of that was worth my energy at all.

Maybe six months later, I built my strength again so I was working with a really lovely client who was hosting a retreat in South Africa; very high-end amazing retreat and safari. I had my flights booked, all travel arrangements were made. It was going to be a big move for me to attend this retreat in support of this client, as she was going to introduce me to her other connections. I felt like I was finally going to move on and move forward with my life.

I also happened to be eight or nine weeks pregnant at the time, heavy into morning sickness, but I thought I'd just grin and bear it for the retreat, and then come back to take it easy and focus on myself and my pregnancy.

Three days before I flew, I went to the doctor to make sure I was fit to travel and that baby was okay.

I found out I had a miscarriage. Within a whirlwind of a few days, I found out that it wasn't just a miscarriage...I had a tumour, and had this cancer that was about to spread throughout my body.

Again, this was telling me to STOP.

I didn't make that flight obviously. I had to cancel all of my reservations. Of course, my client understood, but I couldn't take advantage of those amazing opportunities.

This forced me to embark on a huge health and inward journey. I couldn't look outward at anything. I had multiple surgeries, and then it was a matter of living blood test to blood test, making sure that the cancer cells were leaving my body.

Meanwhile, my husband is a US Navy submariner, who was deployed for the better half of a year at the time. On the submarines, they go "black" so I couldn't get in touch with him, meaning that I was struggling with this without him. Nothing was coming together; every time I thought I could move forward, I was just getting knocked back.

After about six months of constant blood monitoring, I finally became clear of the cancer. I remember getting the phone call that I was clear, and I was in such shock. I couldn't move for a good 15 minutes. I barely knew myself. That period was like a huge reset button on my life.

However...this didn't end the divine intervention that would get in the way of what I "thought" I should be doing.

Soon after, I built some strength and thought, "Okay, I'm going to move forward on something else." I started an entirely new project, in a new industry, that was going to demand a lot of me creatively, but also physically.

I had all these great contacts in place and I had all the right resources and everything was going for me. But then...I fell pregnant! We didn't think we would be successful so soon.

Because of my previous health issues, the doctors and I had to pay very close attention to this pregnancy. It was like I was living blood test to blood test all over again, living for another scan to make sure my baby was okay.

I could only focus on myself and my health. No stress, no over-exerting myself. My whole project was put by the wayside, to my disappointment - but that was just my priority. My healthy pregnancy was all that mattered.

Through miraculous synchronicities, I found myself in such loving support by our local Hawaiian community, supporting me and providing for me not just in pregnancy and birth, but in the healing, nurturing and protecting of our whole ohana to be. We were flooded with love and support - our tribe.

My son is almost 16 months old now - strong, healthy and just the happiest baby. My little wise old man. He was the angel who came to teach me, once and for all, what was truly important.

Every now and then I reflect on the actions that I was "almost" successful with. I think about how silly it was, that I thought they would bring me satisfaction...that they might have fulfilled me in some way. I look back on them and cringe, knowing how much work and strain I would have experienced, and the LIFE it would have cost me.

I sit here typing from my home office, looking over the lush, breath-taking view of the highest mountain on Oahu, and I can laugh about it now. What's funny is that I actually earn more money now, as does my husband, and we have resources and support that we didn't have before - but without the compromises I/we used to have to make, and with a minute percentage of the previous workload required.

And it's as if that transition just "happened".

I barely remember how I created this new life because I barely lifted a finger to create it. It was just there...waiting for me to turn off the distractions, waiting to rush all that goodness straight to me.

My journey to calling thus far, has been a journey of surrendering - becoming "weak". Because that's where the pot of gold was. In my "giving up" and letting go.

My calling was meant to gain strength...I was not.

Clarinda Tivoli-Braun - Ambodhi Alliance Foundation Member

MANDY'S
calling

"In that moment I was defeated on a cellular level. I had nothing left for my old life, I was DONE!"
Mandy Hargreaves - Ambodhi Alliance Foundation Member

I remember the weight of the daily struggle. I was so entrenched in survival, while desperately chasing achievement. My business had become a monster that I had created as I followed the instructions of the "experts" on how to build my dream.

My resilience kept me going yet I was so disconnected, I had stopped listening to myself, stopped trusting myself as I had handed the reins of my life over to the experts. I thought they knew what was best for me, somewhere along the way I had stopped believing in myself, in my own intuition.

Finally I found some reprieve when I left all my worries behind to enjoy a 5 day camping holiday with my hubby and kids. It was a blissful 5 days of laughter, love, peace and delicious connection.

It all came to an end and I will never forget the moment we had to leave to return home. I sat on a log watching my kids enjoy their last swim when it hit me, I never wanted to go back to the life I had created.

The tears began to flow. I sat with my head in my hands and felt a wave of defeat knock over my whole being. The blow penetrated every inch of my body and I was barely able to breathe at the thought of going back to my life…. In that moment I was defeated on a cellular level…… I had nothing left for my old life, I was DONE!

I sat numb, paralysed with grief yet finally I could hear my true self. My soul spoke loudly, " I cannot do this anymore, What the hell have I created?"

Feeling totally broken to my core, I could finally see that ego's empty goal of achievement was slowly killing me. I didn't know what it would mean but in that moment I made decision for change. I gave up the life that didn't serve me in order to find one that did. I felt so fragile at the loss of the old, and yet that same moment I could feel the strength of the new, I just had to let go. In this moment I lost myself, and was gifted the opportunity to finding my true self, my life would never be the same again.

I remember walking around feeling drenched by my self-inflicted shame for weeks, unable to see any value in the girl in the mirror. That was because once I gave myself the freedom to let go, I had to face the truth that I had been avoiding. All the investment into Franchising my business, all the expert advice I had paid for, had left my once thriving business facing financial ruin. I found the courage to see someone to discuss my finances. I walked into a nice little room and met with a lovely lady who placed the tissues next to me as she sat down. I obviously looked like I might need them! I told the truth about my finances and laid it all out there. I was horrified with shame at doing so. It was like bringing a bag of your dirty undies and laying them on the table to be inspected.

I had been under this hidden financial pressure for a while and what I thought was my "resilience" told me to keep going. I now believe this "resilience" was nothing more than my wolf ego in sheep's clothing. I knew it was time to stop following my ego and follow my heart. My family deserved a better life, and I had an inkling so did I! It was time to let go.

My husband showered me with unconditional love, not missing a beat, as I told him the uncomfortable truth. To him, I was more than my achievements. He loved me for the girl I was under all that. I had forgotten who that person was.

As an over achieving perfectionist, I had pinned my value to my achievements all my life. I had learnt to satisfy ego's desires with gold stars and external validation, and was on a never ending pursuit. I didn't know who I was without it.

My ego took a hard hit, yet for the first time in a long time my heart and souls whispers had the chance to be heard. As Wayne Dyer says, this is when my life changed from ambition to meaning.

SO after 7 years of blood sweat and tears I walked away from all of my hard work and declared bankruptcy. Admitting defeat and declaring bankruptcy was like swallowing a bitter sweet pill. Freedom from the nightmare brought with it the chance to let go and start again. Yet I had to make peace with my shattered dreams full of moments that would never be celebrated.

Just as I knew with all my soul I was never going back to my old life, I decided I was not going to let failure take control of my life. I made a promise to myself from the moment I signed my bankruptcy forms. I declared from that day forward, I was going to trust myself and seek my souls wisdom and if I f'ed it up again, I would mess it up on my own terms!

Starting again from empty seemed a mammoth task particularly with the warning light already flashing on my self-belief tank. I was only just learning to listen to myself again, and I missed some of the early signs.

After going bankrupt I met someone who offered me a wonderful distraction disguised as an opportunity! After 20 years of working in Fashion I started working in Insolvency. Talk about workplace culture shock! I was successful at attracting clients and meeting my clients where they were at. I was still in so much pain and I could empathise and support them from a place of love. It was some kind of cold comfort for me that my pain was somehow serving others. Looking back, I believe that working beside people going through the same pain was perhaps penance for what I was still feeling was failure.

I was very good at holding my clients hand as they lost everything however I was constantly told by the industry that I needed to be different. I needed to care less, and well, not be so much like me! I discovered a system ruled by laws which were not rooted in kindness or even fairness. This was an institution of disconnection and I was like a tropical flower trying to bloom in the desert, I simply didn't belong there. I realised that the insolvency work was simply my penance and not my salvation (despite the pay check)

During this whole time I had continued to be a speaker and organiser/volunteer for a charity which held lunches for large groups of ladies. I spoke stories of truth to inspire and empower hundreds of these ladies to love themselves. It was what I knew and what I was good at, it was when I felt like I was really being me, my true self. I was so present, so connected and despite what was going on around me I could always find the strength for speaking message of hope and love. I felt at home on the stage acting on my calling. My effortless genius was like magic that illuminated me and those ladies in the room.

I had started to trust myself and listen to myself and I knew I was ready to leap again. I was ready to birth the value I had found in my first business, value I hadn't seen had any worth when looking through ego's eyes. The value was my effortless genius, which is my ability to illuminate women and help them to activate self-love with their style. I was ready to trust in my evolution and stand in my full self-expression and help other women to do the same. I was ready to listen to my higher calling.

Just as I was ready to leap I was thrown in bed. Once again, I had been too resilient and had held on too long. I was now going to pay the physical price for not looking after myself, not listening to my body. I had time with myself, flat on my back in bed. I now had adrenal fatigue, gastritis and Crohn's disease as a consequence of ego's futile pursuit.

Mandy Hargreaves - Ambodhi Alliance Foundation Member

KYLIE'S
calling

"I vividly remember crying myself to sleep, stoned and drunk with an empty vodka bottle by my bed."

Kylie Ryan - Ambodhi Alliance Foundation Member

My awakening has happened in many layers and stages over the past 12 years and my whole life.

My initial big shift in 2004 transformed me from an overweight, promiscuous, debt-ridden, party girl who drank too much, and pushed the edge of recreational drug use to its limits, to a slim, healthy, inspired woman on a mission. I vividly remember crying myself to sleep, stoned and drunk with an empty vodka bottle by my bed, thinking that no-one would ever love me and my dreams would never come true.

In the one year since my first big awakening, I lost 30kgs, paid off $20K credit card debt, got off drugs, found the love of my life, started singing professionally, and gained my NLP coaching certification to help others.

My first awakening was a realisation of the impact our stories have on our lives. I had been carrying an unconscious story in my body and my life that "no matter how strong you are as a woman, a man will always abuse you."

Now I am very blessed to say that I have never experienced direct abuse as a child, however my family was fraught with sexual trauma and abuse all the way up my genetic history.

Current science now confirms that this kind of trauma is passed down genetically as well as through socialisation. I grew up knowing that the very strong women in my family on both sides suffered and put up with abuse and domestic violence for many, many years.

Over the years since that first awakening, there have been many, many, many more moments of awakening and activation; in an NLP coaching session with a dear friend, we uncovered and released this belief from my consciousness, and it felt like my life had turned from black and white into colour.

I had no idea how much this story had unconsciously affected nearly all of my life decisions and choices up until that moment.

Kylie Ryan - Ambodhi Alliance Foundation Member

calling

"These were my hands, these were my feet, this was my body, this was what my face looked like, this is what my voice sounded like; that I wasn't infinite anymore, that I could no longer be everywhere."

Emma Priestly - Ambodhi Alliance Foundation Member

Ever since I was young, I knew that I was different. I knew that I had a wisdom and a knowing that other people didn't have. When I was young, I was limitless. I spoke from my heart, I believed in what I believed in and I knew that I was going to make an impact in some way. There were so many things that I remembered.

One of the strongest memories was when I was probably only three or four and that was the moment I realised I was no longer limitless and I was in a body. I remember staring at my hands and my feet and having thoughts of "I'm inside here looking out. I can't escape this, this is who I am." At such a young age, I still remember it so vividly. For the first time, I felt somewhat trapped.

These were my hands, these were my feet, this was my body, this was what my face looked like, this is what my voice sounded like; and I wasn't infinite anymore, I could no longer be everywhere.

I was inside this body looking out just as everybody else was inside their body looking out. It hit me that we must all then have a completely different perception of the world.

It took me a couple of years, from the age of about three to five, of having that conversation with myself knowing that others wouldn't understand it; but at the same time, that memory is still so clear to me that I was once infinite and now I'm not.

I knew that this was the path that I had chosen and that my life wasn't going to be a battle or a struggle physically, as there was bigger work to do.

As I got older, and especially when I went into the school systems, was when it really affected me the most. I've always felt there were two versions of me. There was the one that I showed everybody else and then there was the one within me, the truth; yet, I knew that the wisdom that I had, wasn't going to be understood by others for a really long time, so I had to keep it in, I had to keep it closed.

I remember going through bullying when I was in primary school. I was just so done with it. The moment it started, I didn't see the point and I didn't understand it.

It felt so below me and that I was wasting time being a child. I just wanted to hurry up and grow up so that I could be taken seriously.

My life became such a journey of feeling like whenever I shared my wisdom or my knowledge; it was always received so differently. As open-minded as my family was and still is, there were always boundaries and limitations. I always wanted to think so much bigger. I was always telling stories, going to the next level and then the next level and then the next level above that; it was just too far for so many people to even visualise.

I was blessed growing up that I had so much love, support, kindness and love; yet internally, I always felt different. I always felt like a loner in a lot of instances that people didn't understand me or what I was about.

I've always had very little tolerance for small talk, problems and issues; problem aware people rather than solution aware people. I love it when people tell me about their issues and then figure out how to fix it and move forward. They want to discover where the solution lies and ask "how do I change things."

It's always driven me crazy to have to listen to people complain about something but they never do anything to change it.

I noticed that pattern throughout my life where I would just shut off and walk away from certain situations because I felt like I didn't have time for it.

Also when I was younger, there were a lot of things I connected to within the spiritual sense as far as being able to hear and see those that had passed over. I have a myriad of stories of conversations, signs and dreams where I have been able to connect with that but I shut that off for quite a long time for fear of being misunderstood.

When I got to the teenage years, I was very much still on a journey of self discovery and the biggest part for me was I never understood the system. I could never understand why people wanted to follow. I always had this inbuilt belief system where the more people that were wearing a certain brand of clothes or were worshiping a certain celebrity or enrolling in the newest fad, the more determined I was to not to; to do the opposite.

When it came to other teachings within the system, such as go to school, go to university, get a job, work all your life, retire and die, I never understood it. I could never be told what to do. I could never be dictated to. It never sat well with me to have somebody else tell me where I had to be and when I had to be there and how much they believed I was worth paying and that I have to answer to them. I didn't get it, I couldn't understand it.

Yet, living within the system — having the majority of people that I was around, family and friends — that's what was done. I remember doing a 12 month business course, which I enjoyed, then getting my first full-time job. My boss used to say to me, "Who's running this show, you or me?" Because I could always see the bigger picture and if things didn't make sense to me, if I knew there was a better way of doing something, I had to change it, I had to show it. I've never been one to just sit there and go, "Oh well, that's just how they're doing it. They're paying me, so I'll suck it up." It was always, "How can I do this better? How can I be better? How can I make this better? How can this be simpler? More leveraged? Easier? Yet get a bigger result?" That's what I've always been about, creating a lifestyle.

Doing life on your own terms, not being dictated to and being in control; not fearing your own power.

When I was 18 I ended up going into the direct selling industry because for me, that was the safest way to essentially own my own business but not really own my own business. I had a safety net. Going on that journey taught me so much about myself and working with women and understanding the different thought patterns, the different behaviours and the different ways that we showed up in life.

It really proved to me that we're not all the same and that I really am different. All those years of self-doubt and anxiety or not believing that I was good enough was all just mind games. I really enjoyed the journey in the direct selling industry because the mirror that it held up - all the women that I worked with and what was being reflected back to me about who I was, what was important and what I stood for - was on one hand really confronting but on the other very empowering. It showed me, it highlighted to me the areas that needed work within me.

I discovered how much I wanted 'success' for other people. I knew that helping others, in turn, meant that I was helping myself. I became so passionate about them feeling what I was feeling; the sense of achievement, the accomplishment, the capability, the finding of your tribe and having that support but there was something missing. When it came to the recognition side of the business, I absolutely hated and loathed that there were winners and losers.

That you worked all year toward prizes and recognition; yet at the end of all that hard work, the focus was on who's going to be the best, who sold the most, who recruited the most. It was really easy for people to have had the greatest inner growth ever in that 12 months and yet solely focus on not being good enough. It all became warped to me.

All I wanted to do was hide in my own little world, do what I was doing, achieve what I was achieving, the goals the plans that I made with my family in mind; that's all that mattered to me.

I remember making a pact with my husband saying that, "If you and I are happy with what we're achieving and where were going, then let's just not care what anybody else thinks. As long as we're satisfied, let's just do it anyway." After coming to that conclusion, I started to really resent the recognition factor, the competition within the industry I was in. The smiles that were on the faces, the masks that were being worn, yet the women who were underneath truly felt inferior or not good enough or that somebody else was better than them; I hated that.

Then I started to notice, because I was doing it too…the judgement. She did this because she was that; trying to justify why they were better than us. It was like this hidden, underlying current within It that people were saying they were happy for you or they were proud of you, but energetically you could feel the envy, the resentment, the wishing that they had what you had; nobody ever truly being at peace with who they were uniquely. It drove me crazy.

At that point in my life, I wanted to retreat. I was questioning why. Can any of this really make a difference? I was searching and searching for what it was I was supposed to do. How can I be genuine, authentic, real and just be myself yet make a massive impact on humanity?

Emma Priestly - Ambodhi Alliance Foundation Member

calling

"I was internally bleeding and I was on my own. As I lay there, I wondered if the divine source energy was calling me home to the heavens?"

Michelle Cannan - Ambodhi Alliance Foundation Member

The first half of my life I experienced many reoccurring, unwanted life cycles…so much so that I had to either believe I was hexed or there was a higher order at play…for the sake of my sanity, I chose the latter.

NO matter what I did to try and avoid the unwanted cycles, I wound back up in the same scenario, emotionally, physically and financially depleted and feeling alone in the world. It felt like ground hog day.

What I did come to observe whilst in the pendulum of extremes was that the common denominator through-out all of those experiences was ME, so therefore I was the only one who could change WHY I was attracting these events.

In the low of lows I was experiencing bed ridden depression, Post-Traumatic Stress Disorder, major health issues, attracting personal and professional relationships based on drama, rescuing and generally bouncing around in an emotional washing machine of suffering.

In the high of highs I was running successful Acupuncture practices. Working for an airline designing innovative, sustainable wellness and lifestyle programs, traveling and creating memories that still to this day bring a smile to my face.

One of my last trips was to the Middle-East where I had an encounter with a coral reef. I gashed my left thigh wide open. I was taken to a local man who cleaned my wound with pure ethanol to kill the coral, the physical pain that followed was like nothing I had ever experienced. It built to such a level that I could not stand it so I literally ran from it with the two local men chasing me down the back alley until I finally fell to the ground in sheer exhaustion. They kindly took me back to my room where I rested. On reflection the whole experience was a clear metaphor of the emotional pain I was running from.

The next day I was not good, dysentery had kicked in and I was internally bleeding. I was on my own and felt like I was starting to lose my ability to comprehend my surroundings. As I laid there, I remember wondering if this was it, was the divine source energy was calling me home to the heavens when the Bedouins who owned the pension I was staying in came to my room. They had been watching over me like guardian angels

As they entered my room the husband come over to me, I freaked out as I was not clear of their intention at this time. He stepped right back to the door and sent his wife, as she moved towards me she looked deep into my eyes, connected with my soul and I knew I was safe.

They did not speak English, so beckoned me to follow them to their camp fire out in the courtyard. There they handed me a desert herb to ingest, a hot herbal tea to drink and then gestured to me to walk around the fire clockwise three times and repeat the process and walk anti clock wise. They then laid me down and began using acupressure points, within half an hour I was lucid, my dysentery had stopped and the bleeding had slowed considerably.

That night the healer awoke in me.

That night was 20 years ago and the beginning of my inner journey home. I started asking the big life questions with the desire to transform my physical and emotional pain, confusion, frustration and fear of never being or having enough time, wealth, health or love. I was over DO'ing more in order to HAVE more ...yet, never FEELING fulfilled. There had to be another way.

Michelle Cannan - Ambodhi Alliance Foundation Member

REPEATED
cycles

Are you in this transitional phase right now?

Have you become highly aware of your repeated cycles?

And are you watching as these cycles painfully repeat over and over?

Mix this heightened awareness of your repeated cycles, with your naturally burning desire to make a massive impact on the planet, you, in this transitional phase, have woken up!

"The moment of no return - when we became awake and from that moment on, we simply couldn't go back to sleep. Once we're awake, there's just no turning back."
Mandy Hargreaves - Ambodhi Alliance Foundation Member

transition
THE GATEWAY BETWEEN

The Transition is a challenging period of life where our previous motivations start to feel hollow and we consciously begin to create new, more advanced, higher frequency motivations...

We begin to feel a strong pull toward self-actualisation and self-transcendence.

However, there is a lag time between the conscious creation of these newer motivations of self-actualisation and self-transcendence and the creation of new, higher frequency beliefs that align with these motivations.

This lag time is Transition.

In this gateway between "Progression" and "Potency", we are incredibly sensitive. Lower frequency experiences drag us down, higher frequency experiences raise us up.

And in this pendulum swing, we feel every ounce of what we call the Symptoms of Transition[*].

---

[*] *The following list of "Symptoms" is not an exhaustive list, but rather, a representation of the Symptoms most commonly experienced by The Ambodhi Alliance.*

symptom #1 SPIRITUAL AMBITION **conflict**

Definition: Conflict between how spirituality can serve our ambitions and how our ambitions can serve our spirituality.

> *"I was feeling quite isolated and under-supported in that side of myself; that aspect of my spiritual self and my gifts. I was successful yet felt isolated, alone, unexpressed and stifled in my voice."*
>
> **Kylie Ryan - Ambodhi Alliance Foundation Member**

In this conflict between spirituality and ambition, we're highly qualified, we are deeply committed to our growth; yet we're stuck. We're hitting a glass ceiling with regard to the impact we are having on our families, communities and clients. And this is incredibly frustrating.

We've come from this "success", based on society's definition, but this success is now unfulfilling.

We're heavily in our masculine; driving, striving and competing, and this way of being allows us to get shit done, but it's just not sustainable for us anymore.

We want this spirituality, this stillness; we know it's important but we don't want to keep disappearing on retreat, raise our frequency, then step back into life…confused by "how to be", which then translates as a loss in momentum, focus and clarity.

Our desire to contribute, build wealth and influence change, is as high as it's ever been. Yet at the same time, we equally yearn to be the full-expression of our absolute potential…our spiritual self…our genius.

"My ambitious "professional life" was very different to how and who I was in my "spiritual world".

I had strong entrepreneurial tendencies from very young, and so I started out in business at a young age.

In my late teens and early 20's, I also attended a lot of alternative festivals and communes - a whole lot of camping, no electricity, nudity, mud people, spiritual workshops, healing, energy work - the whole "woo-woo" shebang. I loved that world that I played in, but that world was distinctly different from my professional world outside of that.

There was one period when I was a little younger, that I actually did have those worlds merged together - they weren't so separate. I didn't fit in any boxes, and it didn't matter, nor did it bother me.

However, as I grew older, I didn't see how it would be possible to maintain that - to continue to live in both camps - and be successful with it. And so, those worlds - those philosophies and those circles of friends - grew apart from each other. They became very separate, and I "hid" them from each other.

Society told me that those vastly different worlds couldn't merge. I couldn't be spiritually inclined, AND make a profit as well.

I felt like I would have been viewed as a traitor to be interested in any financial gain, and then in this very professional space I couldn't be seen to be free-loving and talking about energy and aura's.

I needed to choose just one road to take, and so I felt I had to make the "responsible" decision.

I continued on like that, and for many years in business, I was not in full expression of that spiritual side of myself.

There was one moment I remember that was really significant for me.

I was on a train somewhere in Sydney CBD. It was around peak hour, so the trains and platforms were filled with businessmen and women. I was looking out the train window and I saw somebody I recognised. It didn't quite register for a few moments, and then it came to me.

The woman that I saw on the platform was a woman that was a regular at all these spiritual alternative festivals and communes I attended - but she was standing there in a BUSINESS suit.

I barely recognised her, as I was used to seeing her barefoot, in fisherman's pants and rainbow-coloured hair scarfs.

That was a really significant moment for me because, before this moment, I had been naive in thinking that I was the only one living this double life - being completely spiritual in one space, and then very ambitious and professional in another space.

I realised I wasn't the only one, and that there must have been many others living that secret life."

Clarinda Tivoli-Braun - Ambodhi Alliance Foundation Member

symptom #2 fatigue OBSERVATION

Definition: Getting stuck in the observation of our un-resourceful beliefs and behaviours (without action).

"It made me feel tired, like I was judging parts of myself, disconnected from my clients and peeps."
Tammy Guest - Ambodhi Alliance Foundation Member

In observation fatigue we've gone from the masculine to the feminine; we've done the whole eat, pray, love thing and now what?

We're witnessing when we're our best self and when we're not.

Mix this, with our natural inclination to take massive action, having this awareness without a "next step" feels incredibly disempowering and frustrating.

"*I have had quite a lot of growth. I'd gone on quite a journey of self-discovery, really becoming aware of my mindset, my beliefs, my thought patterns and I felt like I was really spiritually aware; yet at the same time, was really questioning what's the point of it all when you don't take meaningful action. It's really not making a massive impact in your life and the outcomes that you're striving to achieve. It just felt empty in a sense.*"

Emma Priestly - Ambodhi Alliance Foundation Member

symptom • 3

disoriented
SCHOLAR

Definition: The struggles to fuse our intellect with our inner guidance.

> *"I just felt like there was a gap, that there was something that wasn't right about it, like, I love this, it's great. I'm learning a lot and I'm doing a lot, but there's still something missing."*
>
> **Kylie Ryan - Ambodhi Alliance Foundation Member**

In this experience of disoriented scholar, we are addicts to learning and we see the value in other people's wisdom; yet at the same time, we feel like we're ready to be our own guide; to plug in and get grounded in the guidance we have within us. Then all of the sudden, a sensational book, a great seminar, or an interesting workshop will show up and we'll invest. We are constantly battling between these two needs.

"I'm a person that's very driven by personal growth. For the last eleven years, pretty much since my first NLP training, I have consistently invested in training, coaching, learning, mentoring and personal development on a very wide varied level of the spectrum around mindset; consciousness, activation, NLP, coaching, meta-coaching and theta healing, all these different offerings that have all added layers to my awareness and growth.

More recently, as I've brought out my entrepreneurial side and grown my business, I've done a lot of business training, business mentoring, one-on-one consults with sales trainers and coaches and other people. I am coach, NLP trainer and wisdom activator in the world; so I invest quite heavily in a lot of those other people because I know that that gets great results.

At the same time, I've found that when I was investing - even though there were benefits from all of the things that I've done - there was still a gap between the mentor or the coach's values and my own values.

That showed up as particular strategies that I might have tried in my business that didn't end up giving me the type of result that I wanted because it didn't actually fit with my life, with my values and the level of service or contribution that I wanted to bring to the world."

Kylie Ryan - Ambodhi Alliance Foundation Member

We also find our "personal and professional development" tribes to beautifully but exclusively represent either the masculine (ambitious) energy or the feminine (spiritual) energy. This makes us feel disconnected from the knowledge and wisdom shared, because we're really yearning for these polar energies to unite, to become more harmonised.

> *"It's lonely, I don't fit anywhere. Without this space I was swinging from platforms where it was disconnected and a lot of ego. Then I would be in platforms where it was very spiritual, but not a lot of action. It was lonely and I didn't feel understood, in fact, I didn't even quite understand myself."*
>
> **Mandy Hargreaves - Ambodhi Alliance Foundation Member**

We are also deeply ingrained with the programming that as "Authority Figures" we have to have our shit together...at all times. That our moments of introspection and transformation must occur quickly and behind closed doors.

The impact this belief is having, on some of the world's most masterful teachers became evident to me, during an event on the Gold Coast that was facilitated by Jeffrey Slayter. Everything he spoke of, resonated INTENSELY for me, but it was one particular declaration that struck a chord. He said something to the effect of "I'm both honoured and nervous about transforming WITH my tribe versus behind closed doors. But this is how I want to lead."

> *"What I didn't enjoy was hiding my vulnerability. I think in a lot of situations and our conditioning to date, vulnerability is a perceived threat."*
>
> **Michelle Cannan - Ambodhi Alliance Foundation Member**

When it comes to our business acumen, we know how to make money, we know how to grow our businesses, we know how to sell and how to market, but we feel like more development of this skill, on its own, is NOT going to get the results we want... the way we want to get them.

We feel as though there's another element, a higher power that we need to infuse into this work. An infusion that will truly activate the absolute potential (with more flow) of our businesses...our Soul Projects.

> *"The drive, strive and push aspect was, in hindsight, like pushing shit uphill. I was also compartmentalising my business and my woo-woo or my spiritual side; I really thought that they were 180 degrees out of sync. And so, it didn't matter how much I tried, I just had to keep pushing harder and harder; there was no flow to it."*
>
> **Tammy Guest - Ambodhi Alliance Foundation Member**

As a disoriented scholar, we are prepared to do whatever it takes to make the impact we want to make to create change AND we take this kind of action, pushing the boundaries of burnout.

> *"There was an intensity to me, a seriousness, a burn out, doing it the way that everybody told me to do it"*
>
> **Tammy Guest - Ambodhi Alliance Foundation Member**

EVOLUTION
confusion

Definition: When the risks of evolving, feel the same as the risks of staying the same.

> *"I was looking for yet another business coach and the interesting thing that was happening there was I would find the next course or the next business coach and I wouldn't feel fulfilled."*
>
> **Tammy Guest Ambodhi Alliance Foundation Member**

In Evolution Confusion, we know the shit fights that show up in our lives hold our greatest opportunities for growth, but sometimes we just want to wallow in the victim of those experiences.

I can remember back in May 2014 when everything around me was falling to pieces.

Here I was, in beautiful Byron Bay for my best friend, Danika's wedding. Danika had been by my side, throughout my entire business ownership adventure, and in fact, worked for me, helping me to grow it to an annual revenue of half a million dollars…caring for my business like it was her own.

At the same time, I was standing by her side, supporting her through every step of the journey that was leading to one of the MOST important days of her life.

So much planning, organisation and emotion had gone into this day…a day we had been counting down to for what felt like FOREVER!

But when the big day came, I felt totally detached from the celebrations and disconnected from my role as Danika's bridesmaid.

It was in this exact week that some of my clients were threatening to take me to court…the exact week that my husband had been rushed to hospital with a fierce and undiagnosed illness AND the same F'ing week that my Mum was diagnosed with Bowel Cancer.

Add to this major SHIT FIGHT…the fact that my darling Aria (who was only 11 months at the time) had decided to wake endlessly throughout the night…so my sleep was at an all time low.

It was such an insane experience of life. I knew I had created it. I knew it was there to teach me something. I knew I had an opportunity to grow from it; but I just didn't want to. I was too distraught…I was too broken.

Another internal conflict related to this symptom is our love hate relationship with technology and more specifically, social media. With regard to our learning and the growth of our businesses, we know how powerful these tools are, but at the same time, we just don't feel our interactions with these tools are "FILLING US UP".

> *"I'm sure there are many women that feel the same as I do, that are searching different platforms for the ego and some full of spirituality that just don't find the space they fit and feel like they have to try and change themselves and perhaps even almost be a chameleon to fit into those spaces."*
>
> **Mandy Hargreaves - Ambodhi Alliance Foundation Member**

symptom # 5

TRIBAL disharmony

Definition: A desperate feeling of being disconnected from our social framework.

> *"There was a longing for a sisterhood or a tribe that would get me. It's really interesting that that longing was quite significant and unconscious for a long time; just a feeling of aloneness."*
>
> **Kylie Ryan - Ambodhi Alliance Foundation Member**

In Tribal Disharmony, we know and we're starting to see the rituals and people in our lives that aren't serving us, that aren't resonant with our rising vibrational frequency. We know that we need to either remove these energies, or change the context of our interactions with them. But this is a really scary thought. It makes us feel lost and like we possibly don't belong anymore.

"In a lot of spaces I was holding back and quite withdrawn, even though it never looked that way because I was holding space for a lot of other people."
Michelle Cannan - Ambodhi Alliance Foundation Member

We also feel resentful of some people in our lives. We find ourselves in judgement of them because they're "spiritually behind". This judgement is totally separating us from the lessons, love and liberation these human interactions have to teach us.

"I think that something I was missing, was the level of awareness and conversation around spirit and purpose with highly conscious people."
Kylie Ryan - Ambodhi Alliance Foundation Member

symptom # 6 dancing on the fringes

Definition: A frustrating realisation that we've been dancing on the fringes of our most important, most meaningful work.

"I wasn't expanding. I was contracted. I was playing a smaller game."
Michelle Cannan - Ambodhi Alliance Foundation Member

When we are neck deep in dancing on the fringes, we flow from being excited and energised and activated by our visions for our big work and then we fall into the fear that we're not good enough, that our genius doesn't have ENOUGH value...or that we are putting our family at risk.

But despite all of this, we're still experiencing this enormous pull toward something that's more meaningful, that's really aligned with who we are and what we're here to do.

The week after I realised that I had to either give up on my business or go ALL IN, I found myself on a Skype call with Kevin Nations.

Within the first two minutes, Kevin asked me…

"What can you do standing on your head, upside down with your eyes closed?"

I said to him, "Well, what I really want to do…" and before I could finish my sentence, he stopped me and said (and I will NEVER EVER forget these words)…

"No one gives an F about what you want to do or what you think you want to be good at. You're here to deliver what you're brilliant at, what comes naturally to you. Whether you like it or not, whether it's bright and shiny or not, you're here to do ONLY what you've been called to do. You need to plug into what that is, get on with it or properly walk away."

Stunned and actually quite ashamed, I told him that I believed my genius to be "helping women connect into their true value."

He asked me why I wasn't offering that.

"Because I believe that no one wants to buy that."

Kevin suggested we end the call there, but I'd heard my own words before he did.

WAKE UP MOMENT!

It was in that moment, I heard the whisper "I am done".

I was truly done dancing on the fringes.

On that day, I made a decision.

I was standing at the fork in the road and I was all in. I invested $70,000 with Kevin. And in hindsight, this wasn't just an investment in Kevin, but in fact, an investment to keep me accountable to my decision. My decision of being done.

Done with dancing on the fringes of what I was truly put on this Earth to BE and DO.

Done dancing on the fringes of my absolute potential.

There was no other option now.

There was no turning back from this event - I vowed that I wasn't going to spend another minute serving from my "diluted genius".

new
LIFE!

As uncomfortable as these "Symptoms of Transition" are, I'm delighted to say that they are in fact, a symbol of new life. New life birthing within and around you.

My first birthing experience with my first daughter Avalon was pretty horrendous. I went into acute labor, meaning my contractions immediately began sixty-seconds apart. Avalon was in distress. She was literally drowning inside my body.

I was rushed into emergency surgery, and when she was born, she was immediately taken away from me. It really was quite a horrible experience…for me, my husband, my beautiful Mum who was in the room with us…and of course, my darling Avalon.

For my second birth, I was determined to deliver naturally. I really wanted to provide Aria with a peaceful entry into this world…a rather contrasting experience to Avalon's.

Upon doing some research on what support I could access, I discovered a methodology called Hypno-Birthing.

It's an ideology of being present in your body, transmuting what is perceived as pain, into a peaceful labour and natural birth.

I learned about the period of time between labor and the first stages of birth…

Transition.

It's a time when the rhythm of our contractions and our breathing instantly shifts. I learned that our human instinct when this occurs; is to believe we're in danger, that it's time to fight or flee.

The Hypno-Birthing principles suggest that this is in fact, a stage of labour to celebrate. It's a milestone that represents the hard work has been DONE!

Now when it came to the birthing Aria, I knew when transition hit; everything changed; it was literally like my experience of the world around me had totally shifted.

I was remembering the words of my Hypno-Birthing coach; "this is a beautiful milestone." But all that was going through my head was, "I'm uncomfortable. I'm exhausted. I can't do it anymore. We need to get this done".

I was totally consumed by the pain in my body, and as a result, shifted my focus to the noise of the doctor loudly instructing me to push harder.

I had totally unplugged from the "now". I had given up on staying present and allowing divine right timing to guide me through to completion.

This is the instinct that's kicking in for you.

The instinct that you've got to bring this "transition period" to an end…when in fact, it's an important milestone to acknowledge.

Just like the pain in my body and doctor's loud instructions tricked me into believing I was in "danger", the noise flowing from your television screen, inbox and social media feeds is attempting to trick you into believing you have voids that need filling…that you're broken.

"I was disempowered by the belief there was always something missing within me and that there was always something I wasn't doing or wasn't achieving."
Emma Priestly - Ambodhi Alliance Foundation Member

This is a total illusion.
You are far from "being broken or incomplete".

"It's so liberating to know that I'm not broken and there's nothing to fix; that expansion is why we're here."
Simone Outteridge - Ambodhi Alliance Foundation Member

And despite feeling the most out of alignment than ever before, these Symptoms of Transition are a sign that you're rising into the most profound phase of life; your Life Theme of Potency.

But before we lead you down this path of exponential growth and potent impact, you need to make a very important decision.

Do you want to rise up into your absolute potential?

OR…

Do you wish to continue swinging back and forth in "Transition"?

Every afternoon, I walk down the side of Grandma and Da's house, quietly open the side gate, sneak into the backyard and surprise Aria, who's always busy playing with her 14 cousins.

I love having the freedom and the time to invest in this very important work, however, I am equally blissed out on bookending my work days with my precious family.

Everyday, after I appear around the side of the house and meet Aria's gaze…I receive a huge running cuddle accompanied by the high pitched smiley sound of "Mummy….".

And like clockwork, her next words are "…can you push me on the swing?".

Now, Aria is 3 and she is a very clever girl. She knows how to swing on a swing all on her own. In fact, thanks to her sister and cousins teaching her…she's known how to swing on her own for a very long time.

However, right now, Aria chooses to believe that if she doesn't have someone else push her, she can't go as high, she can't go as fast AND most importantly, she can't bring her swinging to an immediate stop.

Aria…my darling Aria (just like Avalon) has this beautiful expectation, that whatever they want…they must have…NOW.

So when there's no one to help Aria, her desire to STOP NOW and her belief that she can't do it on her own, sometimes leaves her frustratingly coming to a _slow progressive stop_ (and when this happens, the whole freaking neighbourhood hears all about it).

Our experience of Transition is just like Aria's experience on the swing.

When we're in Transition, we have clear, strong <u>motivations</u>, yet our beliefs are temporarily out of alignment with these motivations.

And this misalignment causes us to be at the mercy of the external forces around us; thrusting us IN and OUT of flow and resistance…

IN and OUT of growth and stagnation.

IN and OUT of "the transitional gateway" between our previous Life Theme of Progression and our future Life Theme of Potency.

If you're reading this book, then like us, bringing this period of Transition to a decisive end is THE ONE AND ONLY option.

So to do this swiftly and permanently, we invite you to do what we have done…

Consciously recalibrate your belief system in alignment with your desire of self-actualisation and self-transcendence.

TIME
TO
align

"The absolute truth is, the women who were fully aligned with this process, were experiencing the most unimaginable leaps of growth...growth within their internal world, that was organically manifesting as POTENT IMPACT in their external world."

We know that our beliefs shape our thoughts, actions and of course, our results (Icek Ajzen's Theory Of Planned Behaviour, 1967).

However, as a result of uncovering the Life Theme phenomenon, it became obvious to me, that we needed to shift our "personal and professional development" beyond mainstream ideologies.

In 2014, after spending 3-days in Las Vegas with Toby Alexander, one of the world's most unorthodox spiritual teachers,

I became exposed to a marvellously alternate reconstruction of Ajzen's Theory.

Here I was, seated comfortably on a beautiful couch in one of the private deluxe suites at The Wynn Hotel & Towers. In front of me, were floor to ceiling windows that perched us so high above the colossal concrete jungle, that we could gaze upon the desert mountains lining the city limits.

Next to me, were some of the world's most effectual teachers, healers and leaders, including a powerhouse Warrior Sage, Satyen Raja.

Together we spent 3 days inside this suite.

Toby facilitated energetic clearings…cleansing us of the IDs, entities and thought forms that were handed down to us from our ancestors, parents and "society" (both in this life and lives past).

Toby facilitated Soul Readings, Auric Clearings and DNA Activations and then taught us how to facilitate these Clearings, Activations and Readings for others.

Throughout these 3-days, Toby also stepped us through what he believed to be occurring in the world, concerning the rising consciousness of the masses, the light, the dark and most significantly, what he believed we needed to know, in order to make a compelling contribution to the ascension of humanity.

Toby told us how "shallow" the work is, when we focus purely on "beliefs". Sharing story after story of the people who had risen to a whole new dimension of living and performing when they "uninstalled" their Shadow Selves (un-resourceful beliefs and undesired behaviours driven by genetic, epigenetic programming).

We discussed the importance of "higher sensory perception" OR guidance received from Higher Self. And how we can "tune into" our "higher sensory perception" more often and with more ease, when our old, outdated "genetic and epigenetic" programming is "switched off".

During these 3-days, I was privileged to take part in incredibly enlightened discussions with this extraordinary group of light-workers. And it was one particular conversation I had with Satyen, at 1am, over a fusion feast of Japanese Spanish tapas, that caused me to extract the chunkiest piece of gold from Toby's training.

Everything I had heard that week was powerful, intriguing and absolutely worthy of accepting as truth. But it was this one intriguing piece of wisdom that penetrated my awareness… hitting me with a sense of far-reaching responsibility;

> *We are not broken.*
> *It's just our DNA template that is TEMPORARILY fractured.*
> *Our "Shadow Selves" are these fractures, manifested.*
> *When we SEE these Shadows, we can heal these fractures.*
> *And when we heal these fractures, we can become our absolute potential.*

Fast forward 12-months, and here I was, ALL IN on fulfilling what I believed to be, my divinely assigned responsibility.

It was now August 2015. I had carefully gathered a beautiful mix of game-changing women whom were yearning to realise their absolute potential.

I had created a simple process that became the context with which, we connected and interacted.

We shined a BIG ASS light of consciousness on our "Shadow Selves". Then, in real-time, with NO filters, NO judgement AND with raw vulnerably, shared the emotions, triggers and "stories" observed within these moments.

As we became more competent at this process...we began to translate these observations into guidance AND new (higher frequency) beliefs, thoughts and behaviours, via another quick and simple process I call "Popping".

On this particular day, I can remember staring at my computer screen, both bewildered and ecstatic!

I was in complete AWE at the mystifying power that was beaming from the group of women I had gathered.

As I read through the "deep dives" of observation and illuminating pops of wisdom we had shared, I realised that my intuitive trust in this "idea" was being rewarded.

The women who were fully aligned with this process, were experiencing the most unimaginable leaps of growth...growth within their internal world, that was organically manifesting as POTENT IMPACT in their external world.

These women, who had spent many years driven by the need to contribute (AND be acknowledged), had shifted their focus from <u>making</u> an impact...to <u>BEING</u> impacted.

This subtle but monumental flip was causing them to, ironically, make an impact that was far more POTENT and effortless, than the impact they WERE making <u>before</u> this shift.

Since birthing The Ambodhi Alliance, the girls have shared many stories of "miraculous" outcomes, that have resulted from this "extraordinary collaboration". And one of my ALL TIME favourites is one (of many) from Mandy Hargreaves.

Every day, Mandy goes for a run down on her local beach. No matter what the weather, this is a ritual that Mandy fulfils as part of her "recent commitment" of SELF-LOVE.

Mandy not only committed to this physical practice, but also committed to embodying gratitude with every stride she took.

She speaks of the "gorgeous" people that walk and run on the beach with her. Not knowing them personally, but connecting with them, with a smile or a nod of the head.

Mandy knew this ritual of self-love impacted her and those around her, but underestimated just how potently, UNTIL...

"WOW WOW WOW..."
Have to share a note I received on my car today.

"Smiling runner. I want to thank you for helping me want to live again. You persisted with me, a complete stranger. No matter how hard I frowned at you, you always smiled and said good morning. Then I started to smile back and it felt good, I started to feel happy. I was only here on holiday I may never see your lovely smile again, but I will always remember it. This changed my life as I had thoughts I didn't want to live anymore. Now I feel good about going home and making a fresh start. Thank you. Keep smiling!"

Sitting on top of the world! In awe of all that is in front of me. How totally blessed am I."

Mandy Hargreaves - Ambodhi Alliance Foundation Member[*]

So here I was, sitting with the realisation that Mandy and the other Ambodhi Alliance members, were mastering exponential growth, while at the same time, organically making a potent impact.

Upon digging into the intricate wiring of the women WHO WERE manifesting this constant and consistent growth, I discovered a stunning collective characteristic.

We, as a collaboration of ambitious, awakened women were co-creating a "potently alternate" reality, based on a rare and sophisticated combination of beliefs.

A remarkable belief system, that was vibrationally resonant with our motivations of self-actualisation and self-transcendence.

A belief system that when embodied, bought our "Transition" to an end.

Through meaningful conversations, vulnerable breakdowns and courageous leaps into the unknown, I identified the alchemy of beliefs that shifted us out of Transition...and into a lifestyle of exponential growth and potent impact.

---

[*] *We could've featured a story of increased sales, a rise in profits OR an expansion in global influence, but I chose this one because it beautifully represents the level of IMPACT our growth can have, during the <u>understated moments of life;</u> the moments when we think no one's watching.*

I'm honoured to share these sacred beliefs* with you. And as you browse through them, I encourage you to mindfully observe the sensations that arise within your body, as a glorious REMEMBERING activates within you.

---

* *This is not a complete list of the beliefs we uncovered during our research. However, they are a comprehensive representation of the beliefs that have had the greatest impact on our growth.*

No matter what decisions we make, or what actions we take, Higher Self's guidance illuminates the path of exponential growth and potent impact.

> *"I feel supported in a way, that allows me to really plug into to my own inner wisdom, rather than always trying to seek the answers outside of myself."*
>
> **Emma Priestly - Ambodhi Alliance Foundation Member**

No matter what decisions we make, or what actions we take, we lean into human experiences that shine a BIG ASS light on the beliefs that don't resonate with our desires of self-actualisation and transcendence.

> *Fear is a new social norm for us. We have made leaning into it, exploring it; we are ALL IN on this new way of life.*

BELIEF #3 big LEAPS!

No matter what decisions we make, no matter what actions we take, we take "BIG LEAPS" into human experiences, that our cognitive mind believes to be impossible, unfamiliar, uncomfortable.

It's in those last couple of reps, when your muscle burns, that growth is activated within the fibres of your muscle.

POTENT human experiences are exactly the same as "those last few reps". It's within these potent human experiences, that we activate the greatest growth.

BELIEF #4

BE potently IMPACTED

No matter what decisions we make, no matter what actions we take, we seek to BE potently impacted by the world around us (the natural by-product, the equal and opposite reaction being, POTENT IMPACT).

I finally came to realise that all that pushing and striving to make a difference was robbing me of the divinely timed lessons that saturated the present moment.

BELIEF #5 **open** -SOURCING

No matter what decisions we make, no matter what actions we take, exponential growth is activated by vulnerable sharing and mindful witnessing (in real time) of our transformational processes.

> *"There's been a huge acceleration of my growth by being able to witness and celebrate other women's growth. It's that rising tide lifts all ships; as each of us grows, we each lift each other up."*
>
> **Kylie Ryan - Ambodhi Alliance Foundation Member**

BELIEF # 6 perfection

No matter what decisions we make, no matter what actions we take, the outcome is perfect and full of guidance.

"I trust that divine guidance and divine timing now. I go down that path I've never been down and trust everything will work out the way it needs to."

Emma Priestly, Ambodhi Foundation Member

LOCAL humanity

BELIEF #7

No matter what decisions we make, no matter what actions we take, our contribution to the healing of humanity occurs first, with our local humanity (the humans around us, in every moment, of every day).

> *"It's a beautiful thing to see not only my ripple, but the ripple effect of everybody in this space and their people, communities, families and businesses; collectively we thrive."*
>
> **Tammy Guest - Ambodhi Alliance Foundation Member**

No matter what decisions we make, no matter what actions we take, we plug into a transcendent level of courage and resilience before we take our BIG LEAPS.

I love being apart of The Ambodhi Alliance because it's a collective consciousness made up of humans who are just like me...who are all in just like me. These women are vulnerably and courageously taking big leaps into their most meaningful work.

Everyday, I am blissed out with the KNOWING that the women who are standing beside me, are prepared to take the same risks and are prepared to support me and one another in that quest.

WISE Woman

No matter what decisions we make, no matter what actions we take, we create deep connections with our other "life tribes" when our wise woman is fully supported.

> "I have amazing friends, amazing family, amazing husband, amazing children and so much love in my life, and there was a part of me that felt isolated, alone and misunderstood. That wasn't anything to do with any of the other people, as it never is, it was something within myself that I didn't have supported. And now I do."
>
> **Kylie Ryan - Ambodhi Alliance Foundation Member**

BELIEF #10

transcendent
SOCIAL REALITY

No matter what decisions we make, no matter what actions we take, we co-create exponential growth when we collectively embody this alternate belief system.

> *"Most recently in discovering Ambodhi and the power of conscious group intention, I have been activated to deeper and deeper awareness of the potential each one of us has to create miracles in our lives, and how important it is that we do so."*
>
> **Kylie Ryan - Ambodhi Alliance Foundation Member**

CURRENT

No matter what decisions we make, no matter what actions we take, we are aware of the specific people, places, events and things that collectively support our "invisible current" (flow).

"In this space, I have people that support me, that help me activate my own wisdom, that really help me to shift my perception, that show me other ways that things can be done, help me to work it out, help me to be the best expert for me and to follow the best path for me."

Mandy Hargreaves - Ambodhi Foundation Member

BELIEF #12½ intersecting

No matter what decisions we make, no matter what actions we take, the pinnacle of our value is where our Higher Self's guidance intersects our Genius.

> *"I was dancing on the fringes of my big work. And now, being a part of this collaboration has ignited within in me the ability to uncover my true value AND a belief that I have the capacity to do this big work - that I must do it. I realise that I have to dive in, I have to share this with everyone; not limit myself to just dancing on the fringes."*
>
> **Mandy Hargreaves - Ambodhi Alliance Foundation Member**

BELIEF #13 fusion

No matter what decisions we make, no matter what actions we take, we fuse our spiritual work with our conventional business growth practices.

A rise in revenue and/or profitability is not an unusual experience as a result of our interactions. Although it's not the focus, it is undeniably affected in a very positive way.

EXPANDED
awareness

No matter what decisions we make, no matter what actions we take, we are committed to mastering Expanded Awareness.

> *"Of being focused and yet so aware to everything around you, pulling in awareness and attention of everything that gives you more at your disposal...more energy and more intelligence."*
>
> **Clarinda Tivoli-Braun - Ambodhi Alliance Foundation Member**

BELIEF #115

No matter what decisions we make, no matter what actions we take, we extract the absolute potential from our training, coaching and mentoring by filtering our learning through Higher Self's guidance.

I don't want to proclaim that up-skilling is futile. As change-makers, intellectually expanding is absolutely necessary. However, I DO believe that before we invest in acquiring more knowledge, we MUST strengthen our divine perception.

BELIEF #16 vulnerability

No matter what decisions we make, no matter what actions we take, we receive the lessons contained within our "shadow selves" when we vulnerably, transparently and fully express how they show up. No filters, no judgement.

"What I didn't enjoy before, was hiding my vulnerability. I think in a lot of situations and our conditioning to date, vulnerability is a perceived threat. And when I'm holding space for a lot of other people, I was yearning to be able to go in and have that space held for me. Having this now, is so significant to me because is supports my processes in a way that allows me to then go out and be a more expanded, better version of myself for others."

Michelle Cannan - Ambodhi Alliance Foundation Member

pedestals

No matter what decisions we make, no matter what actions we take, learning from our teachers' hindsight or from a guru standing on a pedestal is no longer our only option for learning.

> *"I wasn't looking for mentors, coaches or courses, I was looking for other women who were driven, determined, action-takers and making things happen.*
>
> *I wanted an alternative to the spaces where there was always pedestals, different levels, leaders and followers. I just wanted to be somewhere that was all equal footing where everybody could help each other rise.*
>
> *Through the success of others, we can really take that inspiration and it activates something within us that's very different to the old way."*
>
> **Emma Priestly - Ambodhi Alliance Foundation Member**

SUBTLE
moments

No matter what decisions we make, no matter what actions we take, observation of our understated human experiences, significantly elevates our potential to accelerate our growth.

"In any given moment, I'm able to access wisdom inside of me that I didn't even know was there and may not have accessed before."

Mandy Hargreaves - Ambodhi Alliance Foundation Member

BELIEF #19 # messengers

No matter what decisions we make, no matter what actions we take, our emotions help us to translate our human experiences into Higher Self's guidance.

"Emotions are the language of the Soul and the messengers of Truth."

Michelle Cannan - Ambodhi Alliance Foundation Member

judgement

No matter what decisions we make, no matter what actions we take, being in judgement of ourselves or others, disconnects us from Higher Self's guidance.

I was so deeply rooted in judgement of myself and the clients whom accused me of fraud, that I couldn't hear what my Higher Self was trying to teach me.

BELIEF 21 MEANINGFUL action

No matter what decisions we make, no matter what actions we take, brilliant outcomes are created via massive action, guided by Higher Self's guidance.

> *"I think that everybody in that space has the same drive to get a lot of work done here on the planet, so we all have that as a common guiding force. That's been really cool to find a place like this."*
>
> **Kylie Ryan - Ambodhi Alliance Foundation Member**

BELIEF #22

feed
OUR NEEDS

No matter what decisions we make, no matter what actions we take, consciously and simultaneously feeding <u>all</u> the needs of our Ego (Love, Significance, Variety, Safety, Contribution, Growth), supports the process of translating Higher Self's guidance into tangible outcomes.

For a long time, I believed my need for variety was strange and unacceptable because that's how it was judged by my family, friends and peers. Now I know that I was simply feeding a "part" of me that was a fundamental cog in my manifesting wheel.

BELIEF #23

love
EGO

No matter what decisions we make, no matter what actions we take, we love and accept all aspects of our Ego (Creator) Self, i.e., our thoughts, behaviours and our physical form.

Ego gets such a bad wrap. But she's freaking powerful. She's creative. She hustles like a mofo...she gets shit done. If our impact is to manifest in physical form, we MUST love and support her! We must make her feel part of the team.

BELIEF #24 PRECIOUS **time**

No matter what decisions we make, no matter what actions we take, we are grateful for this present moment.

"I'm not afraid of running out of time. I am concerned with making the most powerful impact I can in the time I have, and the only way I can be powerful is by being fully present to the only moment I really have, NOW. "

Kylie Ryan - Ambodhi Alliance Foundation Member

HIGH-
leverage

No matter what decisions we make, no matter what actions we take, the investments we make in our personal and professional growth are highly leveraged.

"We have all invested at a very high level in our personal and professional growth - we've engaged the help of mentors, masterminds, training programs, books, courses...most of us have spent upwards of $100K in self-improvement, entrepreneurship, and various other fields.

While these investments are not just beneficial - but crucial - we haven't yet had the opportunity to invest our money into a system, that is made FOR US and BY US, that supports us fully, where 80% of funds go directly back into this system (e.g. development and maintenance of the digital platform; scientific analysis of patterns of consciousness, rewards, gifts, retreat hosting costs, administration teams, special guest healers, speakers, teachers etc.).

We have essentially become angel investors in our own personal and professional growth AND SIMULTANEOUSLY in the growth of ALL of these amazing ambitious women combined.

Financially, we are pooling together - we are collaborating our resources for the betterment of all of us. It's no surprise that women step into this space, without the intention of increasing their bottom line, and yet, end up with such a result, that we consider to be natural byproduct."

Clarinda Tivoli-Braun - Ambodhi Alliance Foundation Member

BELIEF #26

No matter what decisions we make, no matter what actions we take, we integrate technology into our spiritual practice.

Meaning that the techniques and resources that we leverage today, in order to exponentially accelerate our growth and make a potent impact, may have little influence on how we grow and make potent impact tomorrow.

alignment

Most of all, no matter what decisions we make, no matter what actions we take, we realise our absolute potential when we align our internal resources (guidance and cognition) with our external resources (physical form and environment).

These beliefs really are, the bridge that carried us through the transitional gateway and allowed us to gaze upon our next dimension of living...

our Life Theme of Potency.

potency

Our Life Theme of "Potency" is a profound period of life, when we manifest our desires of self-actualisation and self-transcendence.

> *"Self-Actualisation is to realise one's potential. Self-Transcendence is to help others realise their potential."*
>
> **Abraham Maslow**

Within this Life Theme...

- our belief system is beautifully aligned with our desires of self-actualisation and self-transcendence,
- we attract into our reality, the highest frequency people, places, events and things AND...
- we manifest daily experiences of exponential growth and potent impact.

Imagine a life, where you effortlessly influence meaningful change within people, places, events and/or things, in a way that powerfully serves humanity.

Where you effortlessly translate your wisdom into accelerated growth and the actualisation of your ambitions.

Where you manifest, grow and impact along the path of least resistance, still digging in, still hustling but with more peace, ease and grace.

Of being focused and yet so aware of everything that gives more at your disposal...more energy and more intelligence.

This is how we experience our Life Theme of Potency.

Our human experience of "Potency" is soaked with...

Clarity

We have total clarity of our big meaningful work.

> *"I see the importance of my mission, I know what it is and see clearly who I'm here to serve."*
> **Emma Priestly - Ambodhi Alliance Foundation Member**

> *"My head is much clearer now, I'm a lot more determined, I know where I'm going, I've realised that I'm the centre my world and I have the ability to make things happen whatever that might be."*
> **Rochelle Holland - Ambodhi Alliance Foundation Member**

Purpose

We are SMACK BANG in the middle of our big, most meaningful work.

"I love that quote by Marianne Williamson, "When we allow our light to shine, we silently give permission to others for their light to shine as well."

When I'm not in my work, my light is dimming. It's not shining and it doesn't allow all those other little lighthouses around to shine theirs (which I think is the bliss of being a collective like this). When we can stand up and shine, everybody else is led to stand up and shine their light too."

Tammy Guest - Ambodhi Alliance Foundation Member

"I know that what I have to offer is truly valuable now and it is something that everybody needs."

Rochelle Holland - Ambodhi Alliance Foundation Member

Peaceful Ambition

We are feeling more peace in our lives, while at the same time, our ambitions are highly charged.

Full Expression

We have beautifully re-aligned our businesses, so that our natural genius is fully expressed.

"I am now merging of all of my gifts and all of my talents into a potent creation."

Kylie Ryan - Ambodhi Alliance Foundation Member

"Now, I have the opportunity to see my genius and how I can deliver it to the world, so I can create the ripple effect that I always wanted."

Tammy Guest - Ambodhi Alliance Foundation Member

Immense Courage

We're consistently and courageously taking "Big Leaps".

"What has specifically changed in my life is my expansion to show up, full permission. I am now absolutely playing a bigger game"

Michelle Cannan - Ambodhi Alliance Foundation Member

Deep Connection

We're feeling deeply connected to the people and places around us.

"Now, the things that I create and the connection that I have with my clients and my peeps, comes from my heart space and comes from a place where I can truly be me rather than what I thought I had to be in this business world.

I am now BEING my whole self, rather than shunning and cutting off parts of me from the world.

This allows me to shine in my whole self; and this has had a flow on effect not only on my business, but on my family, my community of friends and all of the people I reach."

Tammy Guest - Ambodhi Alliance Foundation Member

Divine Sight

We're mastering the art of plugging in to our Higher Self's guidance; the symbols, gifts and lessons sitting within the subtle, every day human experiences.

> *"Third eye opening big time! I am experiencing a significant ramp up in receiving spiritual guidance. Every day, just about - whereas it used to be once every month or 2. And not little messages. Like, really big friggin profound what-I-need-to-hear-at-exactly-the-time-I-need-it type of messages."*
> **Clarinda Tivoli-Braun - Ambodhi Alliance Foundation Member**

Epic Strength

Fear is now a trigger for growth rather than a precursor to doubt, procrastination and contradiction.

> *"Inspiration. They are willing to step out of the comfort zone and into an uncomfortable space and take the risk to be seen, to show themselves and accept everything that comes with it. By them doing that, it then gives me the confidence to do the same thing."*
> **Simone Outteridge - Ambodhi Alliance Foundation Member**

Accelerated Growth

We're creating growth at a highly accelerated rate.

"There's been huge acceleration in my personal and spiritual growth that has happened with ease, grace and with a sense of effortlessness that hadn't been present before."
Kylie Ryan - Ambodhi Alliance Foundation Member

"I am continually bettering my best, consistently improving."
Emma Priestly - Ambodhi Alliance Foundation Member

Efficiency

We understand how our internal work is translating into results in our external world.

"I can actually bear witness to how quickly I am growing. And when these exponential leaps of growth occur. I can witness it in real time. I can measure it in real time. The efficiency in how I operate, show up in life, is phenomenal."
Amber McLean - Ambodhi Alliance Foundation Member

We're also more efficient at noticing when we've fallen into our "old programming".

"I used to be dancing on the fringes of my meaningful work and I have the beautiful experience of now dancing deep within it. I am now also aware of when I am dancing on the outskirts of it...I know the difference."
Tammy Guest - Ambodhi Alliance Foundation Member

When we fall down, we re-calibrate; we realign really quickly. And our big decisions are being made with ease.

"The planning, actions and results come so much easier, with less strain, with enjoyment, spontaneity even. And confidence in that unpredictability because it's proven to bring me good results. Minus the BS."
Clarinda Tivoli-Braun - Ambodhi Alliance Foundation Member

Feelings of anger and sadness show up with far less charge now and we're leveraging these emotions to accelerate our growth.

"I transform frustrations, resistance into wisdom very quickly and very effortlessly. I can very quickly shift out of a stuck state to an empowered state that allows me to get better results. It's been really cool. It's had a very profound shift in my sense of feeling 'at home' within myself, which then leads to highly conscious parenting, braver business decisions, and a more compassionate intimate relationship with my partner.

All of those awesome things that make life worth living, it's impacted all of those things in subtle and profound ways."
Kylie Ryan - Ambodhi Alliance Foundation Member

We are also efficient at noticing the people, places, events and things in our lives that influence the brilliant outcomes we want in our lives.

Productivity
We know how to translate our guidance into optimal action.

"I'm definitely doing less, I'm leveraging more"
Kylie Ryan - Ambodhi Alliance Foundation Member

"Being spiritual doesn't mean I have to sit on a mountain top and meditate; it actually now allows me to be very focused and very productive in all that I do."
Rochelle Holland - Ambodhi Alliance Foundation Member

Ease

Accelerating growth and making a potent impact has actually become a way of life for us.

"I am now building and marketing a business without the added stress levels. I am calmer and I am more centered."
Rochelle Holland - Ambodhi Alliance Foundation Member

Support

An absolutely fascinating characteristic of this Life Theme, is the depth and complexity of support we need, to ensure we don't fall back into the strong current of our un-resourceful programming NOR the cunning force of the collective unconscious.

As a result of focused, collective observation, we discovered that we were able to sustain our embodiment of Potency, when we *aligned our internal resources (guidance and cognition) with our external resources (physical form and environment).*

That is, when we align Ego, with Higher Self.

AN
extraordinary
COLLABORATION

"We are rare, multi-faceted women who need a rare, multi-faceted support system."

So how do we align Ego with Higher Self?

How do we ensure, that when we step back into "Life", we DON'T fall back into our "old ways"?

Recycling through the same freaking lessons?

And continuing to experience more and more intense "Symptoms of Transition"?

In order to uncover the answer AND as a result of carefully observing my Ambodhi Alliance members, I found an array of other, more complex questions that we needed to find answers to.

Questions like…

How do we create a consistent and permanent habit of leaning into human experiences that contain the greatest opportunities for growth?

How can we embed into our psyche, triggers that alert us to the understated human experiences that contain divinely timed guidance from Higher Self?

How can our practice of Expanded Awareness become an unconscious habit, and effortlessly renders for us, guidance from Higher Self?

How do we "bookmark" moments of consciousness, as they arise, so we can extract the guidance from them later?

How can we quickly and brilliantly translate highly charged emotions (that arise from local and world events) into guidance and action that makes a potent impact?

How do we reward and acknowledge Ego Self for her work, so Higher Self's guidance can be more efficiently translated into tangible results?

How do we become unconsciously competent at identifying when we've stepped out of our Invisible Current?

How can we witness, in REAL TIME, the processing, transmutation and integration of true belief and behavioural change, in women whom are just like us?

How can we ecologically integrate the "leverage power" of technology into our practice of permanently operating within our Life Theme of "Potency"?

These were complex questions, and we were rare, multi-faceted women. So, we needed a complex, rare, multi-faceted support system.

A breed of support system we couldn't find.

And we couldn't find it, because it DID NOT exist.

So we created one.

If you want to "try on" your destiny and truly feel what it's like to exponentially accelerate your growth and more effortlessly make a potent impact, then it's time for us to cease the teaching of our theories and telling of our stories, and instead…

Invite you to come have an intimately personal experience within this wildly unique, game-changing support system.

> *"I can just be having a moment and I find myself going straight to Ambodhi now. And as soon as I type, its like I feel like I'm tapping into all of your wisdom.*
>
> *Suddenly it comes through me, I finish typing and think, "That's not what I expected to come out with. I didn't know that was in there. You just can't do that in another space."*
>
> **Emma Priestly – Ambodhi Alliance Foundation Member**

> *"It creates transformation the minute you go into the space."*
>
> **Kylie Ryan - Ambodhi Alliance Foundation Member**

> *"This is without doubt, a collective consciousness that continually awakens and activates exponential growth within me."*
>
> **Emma Priestly - Ambodhi Alliance Foundation Member**

A destined
LIFE

"Because living a life of exponential growth and potent impact is in fact…your destiny."

I believe it's inevitable that you'll take permanent residency within this Life Theme of Potency.

Because living a life of exponential growth and potent impact is in fact…your destiny.

It's not a matter of IF, but a matter of WHEN.

The beautiful Ivonne Delaflor says, *"You are entitled to a life of miracles."* And it's taken me close to 35 years to REMEMBER this…

When I was a little girl, I yearned to lead, to influence and to make a difference.

I can't explain why I had this strong KNOWING from such a young age, but what I do know, is that it's been programmed in my DNA for a very long time.

And despite unknowingly allowing the collective unconscious to sometimes lead me astray…I will NEVER EVER again forget, that I was put on this Earth to create meaningful change.

This same "remembering" within you, has now lead you to an intriguing fork in the road…

Do you want to continue dancing ON the fringes, or, do you want to go BEYOND them…permanently?

"I think one of those shifting moments is going from desiring, to KNOWING that you MUST live your truth. We simply MUST."
Mandy Hargreaves - Ambodhi Alliance Foundation Member

If you continue to dance on the fringes, I believe you're potentially starving thousands of people of the impact you're destined to make on their lives.

"I don't want to think about what life would be like without being in my full expression of my work. I don't want to think about the people that I wouldn't be able to touch. I don't want to think about the minimising and shrinking I used to do, because I know I used to do it."
Tammy Guest - Ambodhi Alliance Foundation Member

Destiny's a bitch! She knows how to get you to embody her, and she won't let up until you do…

So this dance will continue to feed your repeated cycles of resistance and this resistance will only get stronger and it WILL only get louder.

> *"Your life's work will be lost. The song unsung. The book unwritten. The life un-lived."*
> **Kylie Ryan - Ambodhi Alliance Foundation Member**

However, the fact that you've manifested this book into your energetic field may suggest that you're no longer resonant with "dancing on the fringes".

That instead…you're finally ready to LEAP beyond them.

THE

hidden

PATH

"A path that leads you UP, out of this transitional-haze, and into a still silent space where you can view the timeline of your life, and witness in all its glory...your destiny of exponential growth and potent impact."

I wrote this book, because I wanted to illuminate a path you couldn't see.

A path that leads you UP, out of this transitional haze, and into a still silent space where you can view the timeline of your life, and witness in all its glory...your destiny of exponential growth and potent impact.

And as you admire your soul's journey from above, notice this isn't the first time we've traveled the planet together.

In past lives, we've strived to collaboratively bathe the planet with our magic, BUT it's in THIS life, the world is FINALLY ready to receive it.

We've got really important work to do. AND FIRST we must permanently SHIFT out of TRANSITION and into our Life Theme of Potency.

If you are feeling STUCK in a life diluted in meaning, know with all your heart that its time to stop dancing on the fringes AND deeply yearn to belong to a community that will support you as you make this PERMANENT SHIFT...

Then go to www.ambodhi.org

Let's do this...together.

xx

praise

"Napoleon Hill says, "That third mind of the true mastermind where we each have our own gifts, we each have our own strengths and it's simply through observing ourselves and each other that transformation can take place. That is the Divine Mind that shows up in a true mastermind." Even though I had been in other high-end masterminds and coaching programs, I had never had that need met...until I joined Ambodhi."

Kylie Ryan - Ambodhi Alliance Foundation Member

"The beautiful thing about this space, now that my life, my business, my relationships, health and wealth has all grown incredibly since being in this space, I know that that will continue because this space only allows for growth, only allows for expansion; it's like an unwritten rule that to be part of it, you have to be willing to allow yourself to once again become infinite and limitless and create an unimaginable reality."

Emma Priestly - Ambodhi Alliance Foundation Member

"The Ambodhi Alliance instantly spoke to me of collective consciousness and connection; the food my soul craved. Inside the Alliance my internal world is awakened and nourished to be instantly reflected exponentially in all areas of my life."

Michelle Cannan - Ambodhi Alliance Foundation Member

"This is the first place in my whole life that I've fit in. That's how massive this is for me. Now, I can't imagine my life without this space. It fills a void that I've never had filled before."

Mandy Hargreaves - Ambodhi Alliance Foundation Member

"Abraham Maslow says, "A musician must make music, an artist must paint, a poet must write, if he is to be ultimately at peace with himself. What a man can be, he must be". If you are reading this, YOU are being called to activate, awaken and birth your deepest calling, and you must! The world is waiting desperately for you to be the full expression of your potential."

Kylie Ryan - Ambodhi Alliance Foundation Member

"Its like we all know that we've done this before, that we're remembering and every interaction that we have, activates each other to the next level of our exponential growth. It's indescribable, it's unimaginable."

Emma Priestly - Ambodhi Alliance Foundation Member

I am done dimming my whole self, to fit in.

I am done with separating my business from my woo-woo.

I am done with the illusion of limitation.

I am done with dancing around the fringes of my meaningful work.

I am done with limiting my potential.

I am done believing I have to be perfect, just because I'm an authority figure.

I am done with pedestals and believing "they are better than me".

I am done trying to fit in the "box".

I am done believing my genius has no value.

I am done playing small.

I am done with not being fully self-expressed.

I am done believing I have to choose between my professional ambitions and my spiritual growth.

I am done hiding my vulnerability.

I am done believing that to be spiritual, I need to be still and silent.

I am done with the spiritual work without the action.

I am done recycling through the same lessons over and over.

We are a new frontier of ambitious, awakened creators, innovators, movement-makers.

We have been dancing on the fringes...until now.

We are done.

Are you?

ABOUT THE author

Amber McLean is the founder of The Ambodhi Alliance and creator of the world's first Transcendental Digital Platform.

She is deeply passionate about human's capability to transcend biological limitations, spending most of her life studying the science of human behaviour (focusing specifically on the peak performance of leaders, athletes and entrepreneurs).

Amber is deeply passionate about helping game-changers break free from the shackles of their genetic and epigenetic programming so they can realise their absolute potential and bless humanity with the potent impact they've always been destined to make.

Amber is married to her best friend, Joshua and is the proud Mum of two divine indigo children, Avalon Rose and Aria Anne.